Title V

COUNTRIES OF THE WORLD

Bosnia and Herzegovina

Gareth Stevens Publishing
A WORLD ALMANAC EDUCATION GROUP COMPANY

About the Author: Matilda Gabrielpillai is a former journalist from Singapore. She was a news reporter as well as arts critic for local newspapers and magazines and has edited books on politics. Currently working as an academic, she teaches and researches in the field of cultural studies.

Written by
MATILDA GABRIELPILLAI

Edited by
KAREN KWEK

Designed by
HASNAH MOHD ESA

Picture research by
SUSAN JANE MANUEL

First published in North America in 2001 by
Gareth Stevens Publishing
A World Almanac Education Group Company
330 West Olive Street, Suite 100
Milwaukee, Wisconsin 53212 USA

For a free color catalog describing
Gareth Stevens' list of high-quality books
and multimedia programs, call
1-800-542-2595 (USA) or
1-800-461-9120 (CANADA).
Gareth Stevens Publishing's
Fax: (414) 332-3567.

© **TIMES MEDIA PRIVATE LIMITED 2001**
Originated and designed by
Times Editions
an imprint of Times Media Private Limited
Times Centre, 1 New Industrial Road
Singapore 536196
http://www.timesone.com.sg/te

Library of Congress Cataloging-in-Publication Data
Gabrielpillai, Matilda.
Bosnia and Herzegovina / by Matilda Gabrielpillai.
p. cm. -- (Countries of the world)
Includes bibliographical references and index.
ISBN 0-8368-2329-X (lib. bdg.)
1. Bosnia and Herzegovina--Juvenile literature.
[1. Bosnia and Herzegovina.] I. Title.
II. Countries of the world (Milwaukee, Wis.)
DR1660.G33   2001
949.742--dc21   00--057403

Printed in Malaysia

1 2 3 4 5 6 7 8 9 05 04 03 02 01

PICTURE CREDITS
Stanisa Amidzic: 57
A.N.A. Press Agency: 26 (top), 33, 37, 67, 89
Archive Photos: 15, 16, 48 (top), 49, 52, 72, 74, 76, 78, 79
Robert Bremac: 28, 36, 38, 83, 91
Camera Press: 54, 58, 59, 64 (bottom)
Bruce Coleman Collection: 3 (center), 9
CP Picture Archives: 81
CP Picture Archives/Fred Chartrand: 80
Evergreen Photo Alliance: cover, 3 (top), 20, 21, 22, 29, 32, 34, 42
Focus Team — Italy: 7
Simeon Glumac: 39
Keith Hatfield: 71
The Hutchison Library: 5, 47, 62
North Wind Picture Archives: 10
Panos Pictures: 46
Topham Picturepoint: 1, 3 (bottom), 6, 12, 13, 30, 44, 45, 51, 56, 61
Trip Photographic Library: 2, 4, 8, 14, 17, 18, 19, 23, 24, 25, 26 (bottom), 27, 31, 35, 40, 41, 43, 48 (bottom), 53, 55, 60, 63, 64 (top), 65, 66, 68, 69, 70, 73, 75, 84, 85, 87
USAID: 82
Vision Photo Agency: 11, 50, 77

Digital Scanning by Superskill Graphics Pte Ltd

Contents

AN OVERVIEW OF BOSNIA & HERZEGOVINA

Located in southeastern Europe, Bosnia and Herzegovina was formed in the fourteenth century, when the state of Bosnia joined with a territory, later called Herzegovina, to the south. Today, the country still consists of two geographic regions — Bosnia in the north and Herzegovina in the south. The entire country is often simply called Bosnia.

A land of breathtaking scenery and a multicultural heritage, Bosnia was plagued by ethnic strife and genocide for most of the twentieth century. The country is now trying to recover from the ravages of war and is gradually rebuilding its economy.

Opposite: **The Neretva River flows through Herzegovina, a region of spectacular natural beauty.**

Below: **Sarajevo, the capital of Bosnia, is the country's most cosmopolitan city.**

THE FLAG OF BOSNIA AND HERZEGOVINA

The current flag of Bosnia was adopted in 1998, replacing an earlier flag that bore the coat of arms of Bosnia's King Tvrtko (1338–1391). The triangle's points represent the three main ethnic groups in the country: Bosniaks (Bosnian Muslims), Croats, and Serbs. The yellow of the triangle is an ethnically neutral color. The blue background represents Europe, and the stars, the Council of Europe. The two half stars symbolize the division of the country into the Federation of Bosnia and Herzegovina and Republika Srpska. Designed to make up a single star if joined, the half stars also stand for the hope of a future union between these two entities.

Geography

Covering an area of 19,781 square miles (51,233 square kilometers), Bosnia is bordered by Croatia to the north, west, and south, and the Federal Republic of Yugoslavia to the east and southeast. The country is located on the Balkan Peninsula, along with the Former Yugoslav Republic of Macedonia, Albania, Greece, Romania, Bulgaria, and European Turkey and parts of Croatia, Yugoslavia, and Slovenia. A short section of Bosnia's southwestern border meets the Adriatic Sea. The country's capital is Sarajevo.

Mountains and Plateaus

At 7,828 feet (2,386 meters), Mount Maglic, near the eastern border with Montenegro, is Bosnia's highest peak. The Dinaric Alps form the country's western border with Croatia. Numerous mountain ranges extend from the Dinaric Alps and stretch across the western and southern parts of Bosnia. These ranges have played a significant role in the country's history, deterring invaders and making it difficult for colonizers and religious leaders to control rebels hiding in the mountains. Even today, these ranges are largely inaccessible by road.

EARTHQUAKES

Geological fault lines, or fractures in Earth's crust, lie in Bosnia's mountainous areas. In 1969, volcanic activity caused an earthquake that destroyed two-thirds of the buildings in Banja Luka. In 1992, Sarajevo experienced a minor earthquake.

Below: The Vrbas River forms a steep waterfall close to the city of Jajce.

6

Herzegovina, the country's southern region, consists of arid, limestone plateaus that rise, in places, to an elevation of 6,562 feet (2,000 m). Called *karst*, these highlands contain many crevices, caves, and underground rivers. Except for *polje* (POH-lyeh) — depressions containing fertile river deposits — karst terrain is unsuitable for cultivation.

Quite a different landscape characterizes the central region of Bosnia, where the soil is less subject to erosion, and the rugged plateaus are green and forested. In northern Bosnia, lowlands line the Sava River and its tributaries.

Above: **Magnificent cliff formations flank the Neretva River, which flows across Herzegovina.**

Rivers and Lakes

Six major rivers flow across Bosnia. The Sava River, a tributary of the Danube, forms the country's northern border with Croatia. The Bosna, Drina, Una, and Vrbas rivers flow northward and empty into the Sava. The Neretva River flows across the karst countryside, continuing into Croatia and emptying into the Adriatic Sea. The Bosnian landscape is dotted with glacial lakes and natural springs, many of which support thermal health spas or are tapped for bottled mineral water.

THE WHITE COUNTRYSIDE

Herzegovina is characterized by limestone plateaus on which very little vegetation can survive.
(A Closer Look, page 70)

Climate

Although Bosnia is located near the Adriatic Sea, the Dinaric Alps obstruct the climatic effects of ocean currents, keeping temperatures moderate. As a result, Bosnia experiences hot summers and very cold winters. Its climate resembles that of inland continental Europe rather than the Mediterranean climate of Italy or Greece.

Generally, the northern parts of Bosnia experience colder temperatures than the southern regions. In the northern city of Banja Luka, for instance, temperatures drop to 32° Fahrenheit (0° Celsius) in January. Mostar, which lies along the Neretva River, closer to the Adriatic coast, experiences a low of 43° F (6° C) in the same month. Summer temperatures peak at about 72° F (22° C) in Banja Luka and about 100° F (38° C) in Mostar.

While northern Bosnia receives its heaviest rainfall in the summer months, precipitation is heaviest in the south during autumn and winter.

Above: **Some snow remains on the ground in Maklenovac toward the end of winter. Bosnia generally experiences cold winters.**

Plants and Animals

Forests of pine, beech, and oak are common in the fertile Bosnian region, north of the parched karst wasteland of Herzegovina. These abundant forests have made timber, furniture, and wood products major exports of Bosnia. In the lushest parts of Herzegovina, such as Mostar, fig and cypress trees thrive, together with mulberry, juniper, jasmine, and oleander shrubs.

Wildlife is rich and varied in Bosnia, although the Herzegovinian bear has had its numbers diminished over centuries by hunters. Bosnia is also home to wolves, wild pigs, wildcats, chamois, otters, foxes, badgers, and falcons. Sheep are raised by farmers in Herzegovina, where lamb is the staple diet.

Austrian in origin, the Lippizaner horse was introduced into Bosnia in the nineteenth century. Today, well-to-do Bosnians prefer this breed for long rides in the countryside. The easily trained Lippizaner also enjoys quite a reputation in dressage, the art of training a horse in obedience and precision of movement.

Left: **The European wildcat is a shy animal capable of turning vicious when scared or threatened.**

History

The earliest known inhabitants of the territory that is now Bosnia were the Illyrians, an Indo-European people who had settled throughout the western part of the Balkan Peninsula by the seventh century B.C. During the first century A.D., the Roman Empire conquered most of Bosnia, introducing Christianity and the Latin language. Two powerful South Slav tribes, the Serbs and the Croats, arrived from Central Europe in the early seventh century. They ruled most of the territory of modern Bosnia from the seventh to the twelfth century. A document dating from the tenth century provides the first known reference to the state of Bosnia, which, at that time, extended from the Drina River to the Adriatic Sea.

MEGALITHS

Many visitors to Bosnia are captivated by the megaliths that dot the hills of the countryside. Dating back to the fourteenth and fifteenth centuries, the exact origins of these giant standing stones are shrouded in mystery. Some look like tombstones, while others tower at 6.6 feet (2 meters) or more, resembling the monuments of Stonehenge in England and the Dolmens of France.

Left: The Illyrians, a group of Balkan tribes, were the earliest known inhabitants of the land that is now Bosnia and Herzegovina. The Illyrians were well established in the Balkan Peninsula by the seventh century B.C.

Rule of the *Bans*

From 1180 to 1463, Hungary claimed sovereignty over Bosnia, but the inaccessibility of Bosnia's mountainous terrain left the country a fairly independent state for the first time in its history. Bosnia was ruled by viceroys called *bans* (BAHNS), of whom the most famous were Ban Kulin (r. 1180–1204), Ban Stjepan Kotromanic (r. 1322–1353), and King Tvrtko I (r. 1353–1391). Stjepan Kotromanic added the southern territory of Hum (later called Herzegovina) to the Bosnian kingdom. For a brief period, during

HISTORIC TOWNS: JAJCE AND BANJA LUKA

Jajce and Banja Luka are well known for their rich heritage and important political and economic roles. *(A Closer Look, page 56)*

the reign of King Tvrtko I, Bosnia was the most powerful Slav state in the Balkans. The kingdom declined, however, after Tvrtko's death, and, in 1448, Stjepan Vukcic, the lord of Hum, broke away from Bosnia with his land, Herzegovina.

The Ottoman Empire

The medieval state of Bosnia came to an end in 1463, when Turkish forces captured an important part of central Bosnia, including what is now Sarajevo. The Turks conquered Herzegovina about twenty years later. The Turkish Ottoman Empire governed the territories as Ottoman provinces, imposing taxes and introducing Islam. A large number of Bosnians became Muslims during this period.

In 1875, a peasant uprising began in Bosnia and spread to Bulgaria, threatening regional stability. In 1877, Russia declared war on the Ottoman Empire. To prevent a bigger crisis, international powers decided in 1878 that the Austro-Hungarian Empire should occupy Bosnia to suppress the rebellion and control the political situation in the Balkans.

THE DEVSIRME

The military triumphs of the Ottoman Empire were made possible largely by a system of *devsirme* (DEV-seer-mee), or child-tribute, in which children from captured provinces were taken to the Turkish capital of Constantinople (Istanbul today) for elite education and training. Cut off from their families and converted to Islam, these children of Christian Europe joined Ottoman troops or became royal servants or statesmen in the Ottoman Empire. During the fifteenth and sixteenth centuries, when the system was in operation, about 200,000 children were seized from the Balkans. Some eventually returned to Bosnia as Ottoman officials.

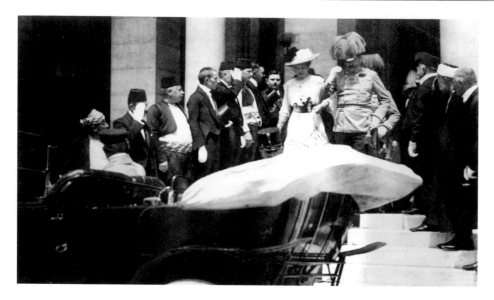

ASSASSINATION OF THE ARCHDUKE

When Archduke Franz Ferdinand visited Sarajevo (*left*) in 1914 with his wife, Sophie, they little suspected it would be an ill-fated trip.
(*A Closer Look, page 48*)

From Austro-Hungarian Rule to World War I

Neighboring Croatia and Serbia struggled with the Austro-Hungarian Empire for influence over Bosnia. In 1908, fearing the growing nationalism among the Slav peoples in Croatia, Serbia, and Bosnia, the Austro-Hungarian Empire formally annexed Bosnia.

In the years that followed, the Austro-Hungarian Empire faced growing opposition from Serb and Bosnian nationalists, some of whom wanted to establish an independent state called Yugoslavia, or "Land of the South Slavs." In 1914, Bosnian Serb Gavrilo Princip assassinated Archduke Franz Ferdinand, heir to the Austro-Hungarian throne. Princip, who called himself a Yugoslav, was thought to have received help from Serb groups. The assassination prompted Austria-Hungary to declare war on Serbia, starting World War I (1914–1918).

World War II

After World War I, the Austro-Hungarian Empire broke apart, and Bosnia became part of the Kingdom of Serbs, Croats, and Slovenes. This kingdom was renamed Yugoslavia in 1929.

In 1939, World War II broke out. Germany occupied Yugoslavia in the 1940s. The Germans created a puppet state known as the Independent State of Croatia, which included Bosnia. The Ustasa, the fascist movement that ruled the Independent State of Croatia from 1941 to 1945, killed most of Bosnia's 14,000 Jews and more than 100,000 Serbs. Two Balkan

Opposite: General Josip Broz Tito reviews his Yugoslav troops in 1944. The Yugoslav army remained a powerful force even after the death of Tito.

resistance movements rose up against the Germans: the Chetniks, who wanted a united Serbian state, and the communist Partisans, who, led by Croatia-born Josip Broz Tito, planned to establish a Yugoslav union of socialist federal republics after the war.

Tito's Yugoslavia

With the help of the Allies, Tito's Partisan forces freed Bosnia from the Germans in 1945. By January 1946, the Yugoslav federal constitution had been announced, bringing Bosnia and Herzegovina, Slovenia, Croatia, Serbia, Kosovo, Vojvodina, Macedonia, and Montenegro under communist rule.

After Tito's death in 1980, the Yugoslav federation gradually fell apart. Nationalism grew throughout the 1980s, and Croatia, Macedonia, and Slovenia declared their independence in 1991. War erupted in Slovenia in July of that year, when the Serb-dominated Yugoslav army sent forces into Slovenia to remove its government. In March 1992, Bosnia and Herzegovina declared independence from Yugoslavia, causing war in the region as the Serbs tried to take control of the country.

COMMUNIST RULE

From 1945 to 1992, Bosnia belonged to the communist federation of Yugoslavia.
(A Closer Look, page 50)

THE WARS OF YUGOSLAV SUCCESSION

Tito's rule in the Yugoslav territories held ethnic tensions in check. After his death in 1980, however, the territories sought independence. The wars that resulted in the 1990s became known as the Wars of Yugoslav Succession. The current Yugoslavia consists of Montenegro, Serbia, and Serbia's two provinces of Kosovo and Vojvodina.

Above: **Construction workers rebuild Sarajevo after the war of 1992–1995.**

The War of 1992–1995 and the Dayton Agreement

Serb leaders intended to make Bosnia part of "Greater Serbia," a proposed union of Serbia and all territories of the former Yugoslavia in which Serbs formed a majority. Non-Serb inhabitants of these territories were to be killed or driven out. In 1992, Serb forces, including troops from the Serb-dominated army of the former Yugoslav federation, attacked Sarajevo and other towns with large Bosnian Muslim (Bosniak) populations. Bosnian Serbs occupied more than 60 percent of Bosnia. As ethnic violence continued, the atrocities committed by Serbs against Croats and Bosniaks attracted international attention. Initial efforts by the United Nations (U.N.), including the sending of a peacekeeping force, met with little success. In November 1995, however, U.S.-sponsored peace talks were held in Dayton, Ohio. As a result of the negotiations, Bosnia was divided into the Serb Republika Srpska and the Bosniak-Croat Federation of Bosnia and Herzegovina. The challenges facing Bosnian leaders today include rebuilding the economy and establishing a stable political and social climate.

HORROR CAMPS OF WAR

In May 1992, Serb forces began shelling Muslim-dominated areas in northwestern Bosnia, causing residents to flee their homes. Most of these residents were rounded up and forced to march in columns to several prison camps established by the Serbs.

(A Closer Look, page 58)

Ban Kulin (?–1204)

Although the title *ban* refers to viceroys, or Bosnian and Croatian rulers who were appointed by Hungarian kings, Ban Kulin took the title for himself, without being appointed. A fiercely independent man, he struggled to free his state from Hungary. He doubled the territory of Bosnia and vastly improved its economy, largely by entering into a treaty encouraging merchants from Dubrovnik, in Croatia, to exploit the plentiful Bosnian mines. Ban Kulin's twenty-four-year reign (1180–1204) brought peace to Bosnia. His successors were often little more than Hungarian or Croatian puppet rulers.

King Tvrtko I (1338–1391)

Tvrtko Kotromanic, or Tvrtko I, was the first king of Bosnia. Nephew of Ban Stjepan Kotromanic, Tvrtko I came to the throne at the tender age of fifteen. During his reign, he expanded the state to include parts of Montenegro and Dalmatia (southern Croatia), crowning himself "king of the Serbs, of Bosnia, and of the coast" in 1377. Five years later, when civil war broke out in Croatia with the death of the King of Hungary, Tvrtko I seized almost the entire Dalmatian coastline. By 1390, Bosnia included parts of Croatia and Slovenia and was the most powerful state in the Balkans. Today, Tvrtko I is popularly regarded as the greatest ruler of Bosnia.

Alija Izetbegovic (1925–)

Born in Bosanski Šamac in 1925, Alija Izetbegovic was educated in Sarajevo. He has been a devout Muslim since his early youth. In 1983, he was arrested with a group of Muslim activists for activities against the state. Released in 1988, Izetbegovic became a founding member of the Muslim Party of Democratic Action (SDA). He was elected president of Bosnia in 1990. In 1995, Izetbegovic joined the leaders of Serbia and Croatia in signing the Dayton Agreement, which ended the war of 1992–1995. Izetbegovic currently serves as the Muslim member in Bosnia's tripartite presidency.

Alija Izetbegovic

Government and the Economy

After the War: A New Constitution

Until 1990, Bosnia was governed by a socialist political system dominated by the Yugoslav Communist Party. After Bosnia held its first multiparty election in 1990, the country had a democratic system of government headed by a multiethnic coalition government. During the war of 1992–1995, however, some Serb- and Croat-dominated parts of Bosnia broke away from government control.

THE DAYTON AGREEMENT

The agreement ended ethnic warfare in Bosnia, but enforcing the peace has not been easy.
(A Closer Look, page 52)

Left: The three members of Bosnia's presidency, Croat Ante Jelavic (*left*), Serb Zivko Radisic (*center*), and Muslim Alija Izetbegovic, attended an international conference on Bosnia in December 1998. Held in Madrid, Spain, the conference brought together the leaders of more than fifty countries that support the Dayton Agreement.

The current system of government was determined by the Dayton Agreement, signed in 1995. The peace agreement divided Bosnia into two entities, Republika Srpska (Serbian Republic) and the Bosniak-Croat Federacija Bosne I Hercegovine (Federation of Bosnia and Herzegovina). These entities each have a local president and a parliament.

An elected tripartite presidency, with one Bosniak, one Serb, and one Croat member, heads the central government of Bosnia.

The presidency appoints a Council of Ministers, which is in charge of foreign policy, trade and finance, and other national matters. The central parliament consists of two houses: the House of Representatives and the House of Peoples. Two-thirds of the forty-two seats in the House of Representatives are reserved for Federation candidates and the remaining fourteen seats for Serbs. The House of Peoples has fifteen members (five Bosniaks, five Croats, and five Serbs) selected by the local parliaments.

Foreign Peacekeepers

In 1995, the U.N. sent a 60,000-member Implementation Force (IFOR) to enforce the Dayton Agreement in Bosnia. At the end of

1996, IFOR was replaced by a Stabilization Force (SFOR). SFOR remains in Bosnia today. The U.N., European Union, and United States, which all helped broker the peace settlement, also play a role in Bosnia's government and administration, providing humanitarian aid to war victims. Elections are held under the supervision of the Organization for Security and Cooperation in Europe (OSCE). OSCE is also charged with maintaining the regional political balance around the former Yugoslavia.

THE OFFICE OF THE HIGH REPRESENTATIVE

The High Representative for Bosnia and Herzegovina oversees the implementation of the Dayton Agreement and reports periodically to the international community on the progress of the peace settlement. The High Representative also supports human rights, encourages the return of refugees, and coordinates the parties responsible for providing humanitarian aid and economic reconstruction to Bosnia. Austrian diplomat Wolfgang Petritsch has been the High Representative since August 1999.

SFOR: KEEPING THE PEACE

The Stabilization Force, or SFOR (*left*), is committed to maintaining the peace enforced in Bosnia by the Dayton Agreement.
(*A Closer Look*, page 68)

Rebuilding the Economy

The war of 1992–1995 destroyed the economy of Bosnia. Industries such as steel, oil refining, logging, and mining ceased operations during the war. Production plummeted by about 80 percent, resulting in increasing unemployment across the country.

Since 1995, the government has concentrated on rebuilding the economy. The urban and industrial infrastructure, including buildings, power lines, and transportation and telecommunications systems, has had to be reconstructed. The work of rebuilding cities has helped provide employment for urban populations, but, with a current unemployment rate of about 40 percent, Bosnia is still struggling to provide jobs for its people. Production has recovered somewhat but remains far below the prewar level of 1990. Along with major financial,

Left: **The Central Bank building stands in Sarajevo. One of the successes of Bosnia's central government was the postwar establishment of a single central bank.**

Left: **A covered market in Sarajevo caters to the needs of some of the city's residents. With increasing privatization of the economy, a wider range of consumer goods is now available in Bosnia.**

banking, and economic management reforms, a national currency, the convertible mark, was introduced in 1998.

Natural Resources, Industry, and the Services Sector

The northern and central parts of Bosnia have prime agricultural land. The country is also rich in minerals, such as bauxite, iron, coal, zinc, mercury, and manganese. Before the war of 1992–1995, agriculture and industries, including mining, logging, food, chemicals, textiles, and building materials, provided more than half the country's gross domestic product. By 1998, however, the services sector accounted for 58 percent of domestic production, overtaking agriculture and industry. Traditional services, such as transportation, education, banking, media, and administration, dominate the services sector. In recent years, however, the health care sector has grown because the war created a great need for health and medical services related to trauma counseling.

Today's Bosnian government is still greatly dependent on humanitarian aid and international loans. Nevertheless, with government plans to increase privatization, encourage foreign investment, train the workforce in new skills, and implement other schemes and reforms, the economy of Bosnia is recovering gradually and will need less foreign aid in the future.

PRIVATIZING THE ECONOMY

Perhaps the greatest economic success in recent years has been the increasing privatization of the economy. Under the Yugoslav federation, all enterprises were run by elected workers' councils. Industries were largely overstaffed and inefficiently managed. After the war, the new government encouraged the sale of state-owned businesses to private individuals and corporations. The economy has grown by up to 30 percent per year in the postwar period.

(A Closer Look, page 62)

People and Lifestyle

The people of Bosnia belong to numerous ethnic groups descended from the South Slav peoples who came to the western Balkans in the seventh century. Today, three major groups exist: the Muslim Bosniaks, Eastern Orthodox Serbs, and Roman Catholic Croats. Many historians trace the origin of the Bosniaks to the Ottoman period, regarding them as former Serbs or Croats who converted to Islam.

Bosniaks, Serbs, and Croats

The Yugoslav constitution recognized Bosnia as a republic of three constituent ethnic groups: Bosniaks, Serbs, and Croats. During the war of 1992–1995, the Serbs and Croats challenged not only the Bosniak population but also Bosnian statehood and independence. They wanted to unite the parts they controlled with Serbia and Croatia, respectively. The war ended with the partition of Bosnia into two parts, one Croat and Bosniak and the other Serb.

Issues concerning ethnic identity are very important to Bosnians. Today, Bosniaks make up 38 percent of the population, Serbs 40 percent, and Croats 17 percent. (All population figures are subject to variation because estimates have been complicated by war displacement.) Since the partitioning of the country in

Below: **This Bosniak family lives in a village close to Sarajevo.**

1995, Muslims and Catholics live in the Federation of Bosnia and Herzegovina, while Republika Srpska is home to Eastern Orthodox Christians. Ethnically mixed villages and towns are no longer common in Bosnia.

Minorities

Romany, nomadic people from India, arrived in the Balkan Peninsula between the eleventh and fourteenth centuries. Today, while some Muslim Romany remain nomadic, others have adopted a settled lifestyle. Another group of Romany converted to Eastern Orthodox Christianity and identifies itself as Serb. In the 1940s, the German-controlled Ustasa killed some 28,000 Romany. During the war of 1992–1995, many were targeted for ethnic cleansing — not as Romany but as Serbs and Muslims.

The first Jews arrived and settled in Bosnia in the sixteenth century. In the nineteenth century, another wave of immigration brought Jews from Hungary, Poland, and other parts of Eastern Europe. Significant Jewish communities were living in the main city centers of Bosnia when the Ustasa launched its ethnic cleansing campaign during World War II. Today, minorities, such as Jews and Romany, form 7 percent of the national population.

ETHNIC CLEANSING

The 1990s were marked by ethnic clashes among Bosniaks, Serbs, and Croats. An estimated 200,000 people lost their lives. Non-Serbs became the victims of efforts to "cleanse" the land of their cultures.

(A Closer Look, page 54)

Family Life

Bosnians value the home as the heart of moral and social life. The destruction of Bosnian homes during the war was, therefore, particularly tragic. Many people also lost or were separated from family members during the war. Some only now are being reunited with their loved ones.

Family life is starting to return to normal for the people of Bosnia. For families fortunate enough to have survived the war, life revolves around providing a better and stable future for the children.

Rebuilding Homes

After the war of 1992–1995, home improvement in Bosnia meant a lot more than just painting a wall or remodeling a room. The shelling and bombardment of houses meant that thousands of families had to patch up bullet holes in walls and roofs and

THE WOMEN OF BOSNIA AND HERZEGOVINA

Unlike their Middle Eastern counterparts, Bosnian Muslim women enjoy a large degree of freedom and independence. Urban women of all three ethnic groups — Bosniak, Croat, and Serb — often divide their time between career and family.

(*A Closer Look*, page 72)

Left: Family members visit a park on a weekend.

Left: Workers reconstruct a war-damaged building in Sarajevo.

THE RECONSTRUCTION OF MOSTAR

After the war, as life in Mostar returns to normal, residents rebuild their city.
(*A Closer Look, page 64*)

replace shattered windows. Others had to rebuild their homes from scratch because enemy forces had razed them to the ground. Still others, displaced from their homes and hometowns, had to settle in new, ethnically homogeneous and, thus, "safe" communities, again requiring the construction of new homes.

Urban and Rural Living

In recent years, urbanization has widened the gap between village and city lifestyles in Bosnia. As more and more people leave the countryside to find work in the cities and to start their own nuclear families, they sometimes also leave behind traditional customs and ritual practices. Urban dwellers tend to be cosmopolitan and familiar with cultural trends in Western Europe and North America. Nevertheless, family ties remain strong in urban as well as rural areas.

SARAJEVO: CAPITAL CITY

Bosnia's capital has an active cultural life and appears ready to put the war years behind it.
(*A Closer Look, page 66*)

Above: **Students attend a primary school in Sarajevo.**

Education

Education in Bosnia suffered during the time of the Yugoslav federation. Although primary education was compulsory and tuition-free, Bosnia had a high rate of illiteracy, especially among women and in rural areas.

In the 1990s, measures were taken to improve education. The war of 1992–1995, however, caused a serious setback to the education of the nation's young. Schools became targets for the expression of ethnic hatred.

Today, authorities are putting great effort into repairing and reconstructing schools. Bosnian children start school at the age of seven and attend eight years of primary school before going on to four years of secondary school. Secondary education is offered in both vocational and general academic schools.

Secular education is supplemented by religious instruction at mosques and churches. Muslim parents may choose to enroll their children in daily religious classes after regular school. Christian children usually attend Sunday school.

Higher Education

Bosnia has four universities. Founded in 1949, the University of Sarajevo is the oldest and largest. The other three universities, in Mostar, Tuzla, and Banja Luka, were all founded in the 1970s. Some Christians choose to attend elite universities in the Croatian capital of Zagreb and in Belgrade, the Yugoslav capital. Some Muslims pursue higher education in Islamic institutions in the Middle East.

Education to Build Bosnia and Herzegovina

On July 28, 1994, prominent Bosnians from all walks of life founded the nongovernmental organization Education to Build Bosnia and Herzegovina. By awarding scholarships to deserving secondary-school and university students, the organization aims to foster young talent, create awareness of the tragedy of war, and promote education as a means of rebuilding the country.

Left: **Students make use of the facilities in the computer room of a secondary school in Sarajevo.**

Three Major Religions

The three major religions of Bosnia are Islam, Eastern Orthodox Christianity, and Roman Catholicism. Muslims form about 40 percent of the population, Eastern Orthodox Christians 31 percent, and Roman Catholics about 15 percent. Other Bosnians belong to minority faiths, including Judaism and Protestantism.

Islam was introduced in Bosnia during Ottoman rule. Today, most Bosniaks are secular Muslims and do not adhere strictly to their religious principles. Many Bosniak men and women, for instance, consume alcohol, which Islam forbids. Bosniak women do not wear veils. Courtship and love matches in marriage have long been accepted, unlike in other parts of the Islamic world, where marriages are traditionally arranged.

Eastern Orthodox Christians in Bosnia belong to the Serb Orthodox Church, which declared its autonomy from the Byzantine Orthodox Church in the thirteenth century.

Above: **The Cathedral of Jesus' Heart in the center of Sarajevo is an important place of worship for the city's Catholic residents.**

Religion and Ethnicity

In Bosnia, religion and ethnic identity have been closely related since Ottoman rule. The Ottoman rulers granted local religious leaders control of key secular matters, such as law and civil administration. As a result, Muslims, Orthodox Christians, and Roman Catholics regard themselves not only as religious groups, but also as political and ethnic groups. The three major religions

Left: **Two Muslim men read the Qur'an, the Islamic holy book, in a mosque in Mostar. Islam is the religion with the greatest following in Bosnia. More than 40 percent of the population is Muslim.**

are identified with the three largest ethnic groups in Bosnia: in general, Bosniaks are Muslims, Serbs are Serb Orthodox Christians, and Croats are Roman Catholics. Religious practice is low among all three groups, partly because of the nearly fifty-year period of communist rule, when religion was discouraged. Observers report, however, that religious practice is experiencing a revival among the young, especially among the Croats in Herzegovina.

The constitutions of the state and of its two constituent entities provide for religious freedom. To a large extent, Bosnians of any faith enjoy this right in areas where they form the religious majority. In areas where they make up an ethnic or religious minority, however, their freedom of worship is often threatened, sometimes with violence.

Left: Serb Orthodox churches, such as this one in Sarajevo, resemble other Eastern Orthodox churches in design and architecture. The church interiors are usually decorated with icons and murals of biblical scenes, such as the Last Supper.

THE APPARITIONS AT MEDJUGORJE

The town of Medjugorje in southwestern Bosnia first became the focus of Roman Catholics and other religious communities worldwide in 1981, when six young Bosnian Croats claimed to have seen visions of the Madonna, or Virgin Mary. Since then, the Madonna has allegedly appeared almost daily in Medjugorje.

(*A Closer Look, page 46*)

Language and Literature

One Language, Two Scripts

Although they belong to various ethnic groups, the people of Bosnia speak one common language, Serbo-Croatian. A South Slav tongue also used by the people of Serbia and Croatia, Serbo-Croatian was spoken in Bosnia as early as the twelfth century, during the time of the bans. Under Ottoman rule, it fell behind Arabic and Turkish in usage. Ottoman rule resulted in an estimated six thousand Turkish words entering the Serbo-Croatian language.

In Bosnia today, Bosniaks, Serbs, and Croats no longer call their national language Serbo-Croatian. Instead, Bosniaks and Croats call it, respectively, Bosnian and Croatian and write it in the Roman script. Serbs call the language Serbian and use the Cyrillic script. Educated and literate people of all ethnic backgrounds have little difficulty reading both scripts.

A Long Literary Tradition

Latin, Greek, Slav, Turkish, Arabic, Persian, and central European influences have combined over centuries to create complex literary forms in Bosnia. Examples of this multicultural heritage

Left: **A Serbo-Croatian sign in Cyrillic reads, "Welcome to Republic of Srpska." Among the scripts used today to write Serbo-Croatian, only Cyrillic has Slav origins. The Cyrillic alphabet was invented in the ninth century by Cyril, a monk who was later made a saint. Cyrillic is also used today for other Slav languages, including Russian.**

Left: A streetside stall in Sarajevo sells books rescued from bookstores that were destroyed during the war.

include a Bosnian poetry form with Arab and Spanish influences, called Aljamiado literature, and Arab and Persian poetry forms written in the Serbo-Croatian language.

Bosnia also has an impressive heritage of folk poetry, including ballads; laments, or sad poems; and epic poems. The lament *Hasanaganica* (*The Wife of Hasan Aga*), a tale of tragic love and misunderstanding, was brought west by an eighteenth-century Italian priest, Abbé Fortis. The lament became a popular folk poem in Europe. Famous writers such as Johann Wolfgang von Goethe of Germany, Lord Byron of England, and Alexander Pushkin of Russia translated the poem into their own languages.

Literature also flourished during the Ottoman period, but many of the original writings remain unknown in the West because they were never translated. During the war of 1992–1995, many libraries that housed manuscripts were destroyed, and these works were lost. Some Bosniak literary writings survive today in collections in Turkey, Austria, and Egypt.

A Literary Revival

Bosnia is witnessing a literary revival in the postwar period. *Scar on the Stone*, a collection of the writings of living Bosnian poets, has been translated into English. Contemporary Bosnian writers, such as Milijenko Jergovic, Dzevad Karasahan, Ivan Lovrenovic, Goran Simic, and Abdulah Sidran, are bringing Bosnian literature, in translations, to readers abroad.

IVO ANDRIC: CELEBRATED WRITER

Bosnian-born writer Ivo Andric (1892–1975) won the Nobel Prize for Literature in 1961. Several of his works are set in Bosnia.

(*A Closer Look*, page 44)

Arts

Architecture

The war of 1992–1995 destroyed many buildings in Bosnia, thinning a visual feast of Islamic and Western and Eastern European architecture and of Roman, medieval, Gothic, and baroque styles. Nevertheless, with ongoing restoration work, much of the architectural heritage of Bosnia still resides in the remaining buildings and bridges.

From the fifteenth century onward, the Ottoman Turks built, at the intersections of regional roads, towns centered around bazaars. Each town's mosque, bazaar, and public bath were interconnected. Bosnia has spectacular examples of Ottoman mosques, which typically consist of cubic structures topped by domes. Larger and more elaborate mosques often include minarets, the tall towers from which Muslim religious leaders call the people to prayer. The Ottomans also left a legacy of impressive stone fortresses.

Left: **A Turkish fortress overlooks a town in Herzegovina.**

Ottoman architecture borrowed from Byzantine and Christian elements. For instance, the Fethija mosque in Bihać was transformed from an existing Gothic church, starting a style of Ottoman mosque construction in Bosnia that featured a spacious ground floor and high, narrow, stained-glass, Gothic-style windows. Similarly, Christian architecture in Bosnia incorporated Ottoman influences.

Above: **Ornate wooden furniture decorates a seventeenth-century house in Mostar. Woodcarving has a long tradition in Bosnia.**

Woodcarving

Timber is an abundant resource in Bosnia, and woodcarving in the country is an ancient craft. Wood was traditionally used to make almost all the parts of a house, from walls to roofs to floors. Furniture, too, was elaborately carved from wood and adorned with floral, geometric, and calligraphic motifs, as well as animal and plant figures. The Ottoman Turks brought woodcarving styles from Islamic territories and the Mediterranean. Today, seventeenth- and eighteenth-century houses in Sarajevo, Jajce, and Mostar feature wooden fixtures, furniture, and wall panelings decorated with carving. Mosques throughout the country have magnificently carved wooden staircases and galleries.

The Book Arts

From the sixteenth to the eighteenth century, Bosnia produced many craftspeople who excelled in book arts. Manuscript illumination, miniature painting, and calligraphy were all highly developed skills during Ottoman rule. Another art associated with the production of books was leather binding. Leather ornamentation was highly elaborate and included embroidery and the use of gold detailing. Today, Sarajevo has an especially strong tradition in Bosnian bookbinding.

Textiles and Carpets

Wall hangings, decorated fabrics, and embroidered cushion covers and pillowcases add elegance to homes and have a special place in Bosnian culture. The Ottoman Turks, who developed the textile industry, built *bezistan* (BEZZ-ih-stahn), or large, domed structures, to house textile and clothing shops. Today, textile manufacture remains a leading industry, offering beautiful and valuable fabrics, such as velvet, silk, and brocade.

Carpet weaving was a household art in pre-Ottoman times. Under Ottoman rule, however, the art advanced greatly, incorporating techniques and motifs from other parts of the Ottoman Empire. The Persians, masters of carpet weaving, were particularly influential in the development of the art in Bosnia. Stolac, Gacko, Foča, Sarajevo, and Visegrad are well-known

MUSIC AND DANCE

Born of a blend of Eastern and Western influences, traditional Bosnian music and dance are still practiced today.
(*A Closer Look,* page 60)

Left: **Beautiful rugs are displayed outside a shop in Mostar.**

centers of carpet manufacture in Bosnia. Workshops specialize in particular designs, and carpets from the various towns differ in their use of color and decorative motifs.

Metalwork

Craftspeople in Bosnia excel in metal engraving, embossing, encrustation, and filigree work. Such techniques have been used for centuries to decorate household utensils and jewelry, as well as firearms, daggers, swords, gates, doors, and windows.

The Ottoman Turks introduced the art of coppersmithing and the technique of embossing designs on copper or silver sheet metal. Encrustation involves carving designs in wood, ivory, or steel, then filling the recesses with silver and gold wires or mother-of-pearl. Filigree work has Christian influences. Known also as "monastery work" because it was carried out by monks, filigree work involves complex, interlaced ornamentation using metal wires. Craftspeople from Sarajevo, Travnik, and Mostar traditionally specialize in embossing and engraving, while the best filigree workers hail from Banja Luka and Foča.

Leisure and Festivals

Traditional Pastimes

Bosnians are known for their warm hospitality. Village life is characterized by the *ide na kafu* (ih-deh nah KAH-FOO), or coffee visit, when friends and neighbors drop by for a friendly chat. Between and after their domestic duties, village women also call on their neighbors to exchange daily news. A special event, such as a wedding, a birth, or a young person's homecoming from military service or from a university, is also an occasion for receiving visitors.

The gifts of wit and storytelling are greatly appreciated in Bosnia. Rural Bosnians often entertain small audiences of friends and neighbors with anecdotes and tales.

Embroidery is a popular hobby among women from rural parts of Bosnia. Embroidered patterns and figures decorate towels, handkerchiefs, pillowcases, belts, women's outfits, and wedding gifts. Many ethnic groups can be identified just from the distinct patterns of embroidery on their garments and belongings.

Left: **A rural family living on the outskirts of Sarajevo spends leisure time enjoying coffee together.**

Above: **Children play in a park in Sarajevo.**

Muslim styles of embroidery often feature designs that wind in continuous paths. The motifs do not cover the entire fabric. Instead, they are positioned in the center or at the side. Wise sayings or verses from the Qur'an are also embroidered on rectangular pieces of cloth, framed, and hung on walls.

Urban Pastimes

City dwellers have access to a wide range of leisure activities. Besides spending time with the family, urban Bosnians go shopping or to the movies, visit dance clubs, meet friends at cafés, and enjoy walks in neighborhood parks. They might also take up indoor hobbies, such as reading and embroidery, or outdoor activities, such as cycling and in-line skating.

In the 1970s, Sarajevo was the center of Yugoslav rock and popular music. Sarajevo, Banja Luka, Mostar, and Tuzla supported professional and amateur theater companies. Much of this cultural life is undergoing a revival in postwar Bosnia.

Left: **Residents of Sarajevo enjoy skiing and sledding down the slopes of Mount Bjelasnica in Sarajevo. These same slopes hosted ski events in the 1984 Winter Olympics.**

Winter Sports and Fishing

In the cold months, well-to-do Bosnians head for resorts in the countryside for ice-skating, sledding, and cross-country skiing. Bosnian children enjoy sledding down snow-covered city streets.

Bosnia's lakes Jablanicko Jezero and Busko Jezero are known worldwide as the best spots for fishing in the western Balkans. Fishing enthusiasts come from all over Bosnia, as well as from Western Europe, to fish in these waters.

Hunting and Hiking

The geography of Bosnia, with its many mountains, rivers, and wildlife, influences the people's main leisure activities. Large national parks and game reserves are popular places for weekend and annual vacations and offer accommodation in the form of hunting lodges.

Hunting has been a major sport in this region for centuries, attracting many foreign vacationers in the early summer. A particular challenge for the experienced hunter is the Herzegovinian bear. Native to the Neretva Valley, this huge, dark brown, plant-eating bear is strong enough to uproot trees and roll boulders to ward off hunters. Hunting enthusiasts also seek out birds, rabbits, deer, lynx, chamois, and hares.

Like hunting, hiking offers sports enthusiasts the thrill of being surrounded by the country's breathtaking mountain ranges, rocks, gullies, and forests.

Soccer and Basketball

Soccer and basketball are among Bosnia's most popular sports. The Bosnian national soccer team was grouped with Scotland, Lithuania, Estonia, the Czech Republic, and the Faroe Islands in the qualifying round for the Euro 2000 soccer championships. Bosnia won three and tied in two of the ten matches played, and the team placed fourth in the group.

Bosnia has three soccer leagues: the Premier Soccer League of Republika Srpska, the Premier League of the Federation of Bosnia and Herzegovina, and the Premier League of Croat-controlled areas of the Federation. Negotiations are under way for the merging of the two Federation leagues.

The Federation and Republika Srpska each have a basketball league. The two top teams (the winner in each league) meet for play-offs at the end of the basketball season. A single league is expected to be formed by 2001.

Below: **Teenagers in a Sarajevo neighborhood enjoy a friendly game of soccer.**

Festivals

The people of Bosnia have three major faiths and, therefore, celebrate a great many religious festivals. With its numerous saints, the Eastern Orthodox Church has an especially full festive calendar. In addition, festivals of uncertain religious origin are celebrated by people of all faiths. Mediterranean specialties, Turkish desserts, and Bosnian wines and plum brandy are featured on festive menus throughout Bosnia.

Ramadan and Bajram

Bosnian Muslims celebrate Bajram during the three days following Ramadan, the fasting month. During Bajram, the minarets of all mosques are illuminated with strings of electric lights. Anniversaries of mosques are also a cause for celebration and attract large crowds.

Christmas

Christmas is celebrated by about half the population, but customs differ from region to region. Bosnian Serbs have a tradition of

DJURDJEVDAN

Djurdjevdan, May 6, is a celebration of spring and fertility. Both Bosniaks and Serbs observe the festival, although Serbs call it St. George's Day. Djurdjevdan is celebrated with courtship rituals and fairs throughout the countryside.

Left: Gazi Husrev-Bey mosque in Sarajevo is decorated with strings of colorful lights during Bajram.

Above: **Serbs celebrate Krsna Slava at an Eastern Orthodox church.**

decorating a *badnjak* (BAHD-nyak), or Yule tree, at Christmastime. On the morning of Christmas Eve, the men of Serb households select and chop down young oak trees. The trees symbolize the wood of Christ's cross, a central icon of the Eastern Orthodox Church. They also represent new life springing forth after death during winter. The lower, heavier portion of each tree is split into three logs. The children of the household decorate the upper, leafy part of their tree with fruits, nuts, candies, and ribbons. The decorated tree is then carried into the home and presented to the host, who blesses it using wheat grains, wine, and oil. Finally, the tree is positioned in the home, and the children place straw, signifying Christ's birth in a manger, under the tree. Straw is also strewn under the festive table and in other areas of the home. The three Yule logs are put in the hearth for a lovely, warm fire.

Krsna Slava

Krsna Slava commemorates the spiritual birthday of the Serbs as a people. Each Serb family, however, observes it on the day of that family's home or patron saint, when the family or tribe was first baptized into the Eastern Orthodox Church. Many Serb families take St. George as their patron saint and, thus, commemorate St. George's Day, May 6, as their Krsna Slava.

Food

Bosnian cuisine is a delicious combination of the flavors of Central Europe, the Balkans, the Middle East, and the Mediterranean. *Cevapcici* (CHAY-VAHP-chee-chee) is ground lamb, pork, or beef seasoned with spices and shaped into sausages. Grilled together with onions, it is served hot on a fresh *somun* (SOH-moon), a thick pita bread. Cevapcici is usually prepared over an open fire and eaten outdoors. *Pljeskavica* (PLYAY-skah-vit-zah) involves a similar preparation, but the meat is molded into patties instead. Another mouthwatering dish is Bosnian hotpot stew, *bosanski lonac* (BOSS-ahn-skee LON-atz). This layered mixture of meat and vegetables is roasted slowly and served in the vase-like ceramic pot in which it is cooked. The ingredients of many Bosnian dishes, such as bosanski lonac, include wild mushrooms (often handpicked rather than bought at the market) and sun-dried peppers and tomatoes.

The Ottomans introduced distinctly Eastern preparations of cooked meat and stuffed vegetables. A tasty filling made of ground meat, rice, spices, and chopped vegetables is wrapped in cooked cabbage, vine, or kale leaves. Alternatively, the filling may be stuffed into peppers, hollowed potatoes, or onions. These are

MEALS

At mealtimes, some rural dwellers still sit on a cloth placed on the floor, serving food from a common pot. This traditional practice is slowly disappearing. Today, most Bosnians eat at tables.

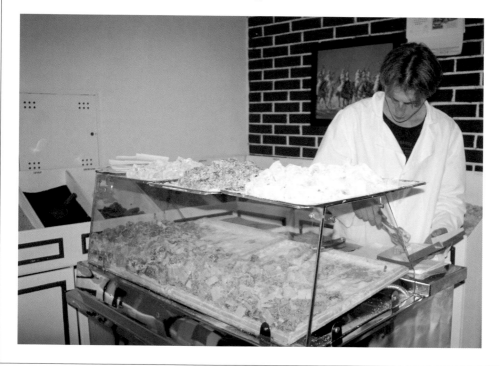

Left: Turkish delight, a sticky candy, is sold in this candy store in Sarajevo.

then stacked in a deep serving dish, tightly sealed with a lid, and cooked very slowly over an open fire. This ensures that the meat cooks in its own juices and the various ingredients retain their individual flavors.

Lamb is the main fare in Herzegovina. A variety of delicious dishes include boiled lamb, roast lamb, fried lamb, ragout of lamb, and lamb soup.

Above: **A market in Sarajevo stocks a wide variety of fruit. Plums, apples, grapes, pears, and pomegranates are readily available in Bosnia. Plums are used to make a thick jam as well as sljivovica, an immensely popular brandy. Bosnia is also known for its damsons, or "Turkish plums."**

Desserts and Beverages

Bosnians eat an assortment of Mediterranean desserts and candies, including Turkish delight, a sticky candy. Baklava is a delicious Mediterranean dessert that consists of rich layers of pastry filled with chopped nuts, honey, and other tasty ingredients.

Bosnia exports brandy to many countries, including the United States. Locals drink s*ljivovica* (SHLEE-voh-vit-zah), or plum brandy, and *loza* (LOH-zzah), or grape brandy. Bosnians also enjoy *kefir* (KAY-fir), a thin, yogurt drink, and *salep* (SAH-lape), a special tea. Turkish and espresso coffees are favorites, too.

A CLOSER LOOK AT BOSNIA & HERZEGOVINA

A country with a long history, Bosnia has experienced occupation by several powers over many centuries. This mixed heritage has created a rich culture known for its literary and musical traditions. Foreign rule has also influenced the architecture of historic towns, such as Jajce and Banja Luka. In recent years, Bosnia made international headlines for its war and for atrocities committed during the war, as well as for the peace process set in motion by the Dayton Agreement. Although the war has left wounds that will take many years to heal, recovery is well under way. Cities such as Sarajevo and Mostar have largely been restored or rebuilt. The economy is benefiting from privatization, and an international peacekeeping force is helping Bosnian civilians resume life after the war.

Opposite: **Many children in Sarajevo belong to youth clubs organized to help them adjust to life after the recent war.**

Below: **Mostar, a picturesque town located along the Neretva River, was bombarded during the war of 1992–1995.**

Ivo Andric: Celebrated Writer

Nobel Prize winner Ivo Andric was born in a town near Travnik, Bosnia, on October 10, 1892. He studied philosophy at leading Austrian universities and received his doctorate from the University of Graz in 1923. He died in Belgrade in 1975.

Andric began his literary career as a poet in 1914. Along with other Serbian nationalists, he was jailed that year for suspected involvement in the assassination of Archduke Franz Ferdinand. During his imprisonment, he wrote *Ex Ponto* (1918), a lyrical prose work. His short stories were published from 1920 onward.

Left: Bosnia-born writer Ivo Andric earned worldwide fame for his lyrical poetry and the solemn beauty of his prose. After World War I, Andric became a diplomat in the government of the Yugoslav kingdom. Andric was serving in the German capital of Berlin as the Yugoslav minister when Germany invaded Yugoslavia in 1941. He resigned from office that year and spent the rest of his life in the Yugoslav capital of Belgrade.

Literary Works

Although Andric's political outlook was more Yugoslav than Bosnian, Bosnia, the land of his birth, remained the primary subject of his literary work and the center of his aesthetic and humanistic vision. His first novella, *The Trip of Alija Djerzelez* (1920), showed his keen understanding of the psychology of his fellow Bosnians. In this work, he presents universal themes through stories of the life of his native province. In *The Bridge on the Drina* and *Bosnian Story*, both published in 1945, he deals with the clash of East and West in Bosnian history. Arguably Andric's best work, *The Bridge on the Drina* earned worldwide critical acclaim for its epic scope and beautiful language. *The Woman of Sarajevo* (1945) and *New Stories* (1948) moved away from a strict focus on Bosnia, but Andric returned to his favored theme of Bosnian history in *The Devil's Yard* (1954). In this work, he presents the experiences of a Bosnian Franciscan monk, Fra Peter, who is imprisoned in an Istanbul jail for plotting against Ottoman rule. In 1961, Andric was awarded the Nobel Prize for Literature. His works have since been published in all major world languages.

Above: The bridge over the Drina River at Visegrad was immortalized in literature by Ivo Andric's book of the same title. This photograph of the bridge was taken in 1961, the year that Andric won the Nobel Prize for Literature.

The Apparitions at Medjugorje

The First Apparitions

On June 24, 1981, at approximately 6 p.m., on a hill in Medjugorje called Crnica, six children saw what they described as an extremely beautiful young woman carrying a little child. The woman beckoned to them, but they were afraid to approach her. The next day, four of the children, Ivanka Ivankovic, Mirjana Dragicevic, Vicka Ivankovic, and Ivan Dragicevic, went to the hill hoping to see the woman again. They were accompanied by two other children, Maria Pavlovic and Jakov Colo. The apparitions appeared again every day for the next five days. The woman identified herself as the Blessed Virgin Mary, spoke to the children about many things, and answered their questions. On the fifth day, about fifteen thousand people gathered on the hill, but the apparition appeared only to the children. On the sixth day, Ivanka, Mirjana, Vicka, Ivan, Maria, and Jakov were examined by doctors and pronounced physically and mentally healthy. Later that day, they saw the Madonna yet again.

Below: **Crowds gather at the site where the Virgin Mary allegedly first appeared to six Croat children in Medjugorje. This site is now a shrine.**

Left: **Souvenir shops in Medjugorje are stocked with figurines of the Virgin Mary, who is said to appear almost daily in the town.**

Since 1981, the Madonna has allegedly appeared almost every day in Medjugorje, not only to the six "visionaries" but also to other people of different ages, races, and walks of life. Millions of Roman Catholics, as well as people of other faiths, from all over the world, have visited Medjugorje. Some have come away converted or spiritually revived, and witnesses have reported healing miracles.

A Message for the World

According to the six visionaries, who are now adults, the Madonna's main mission in Medjugorje is to tell the world that God exists and wants humankind to be reconciled to Him through conversion and prayer. In addition, each of the six visionaries is to receive ten "secrets," or prophecies, concerning events that will happen on Earth in the future. Some of the secrets concern the whole world, while others are of personal significance to the visionaries. Whether or not something supernatural is happening at Medjugorje, the apparitions have had a big impact on Roman Catholic communities all over the world.

Assassination of the Archduke

On June 28, 1914, a young Bosnian Serb named Gavrilo Princip raised his gun on Franz Joseph Street in Sarajevo and killed Archduke Franz Ferdinand, the heir apparent to the Austro-Hungarian throne. His act sparked off World War I.

Serb Nationalism and Gavrilo Princip

In 1908, the Austro-Hungarian Empire annexed Bosnia. In the years that followed, Serb nationalism and opposition to Austro-Hungarian rule increased in Bosnia. Princip opposed Turkish and Austro-Hungarian rule. Some historians believe that the Black Hand, a Serb secret society, recruited and trained Princip and other Bosnian Serbs in terrorism. Other scholars believe that Princip was a member of Mladna Bosna (Young Bosnia), a group of revolutionaries who supported the movement to unite the Slav people in a state called Yugoslavia, the "Land of the South Slavs." In 1914, Archduke Franz Ferdinand of Austria visited Sarajevo to watch the summer military maneuvers of the Austro-Hungarian army. The visit became an occasion for Princip, and the group to which he belonged, to challenge foreign rule in the Balkans.

Above: **Archduke Franz Ferdinand (1863–1914) poses for a family photograph with his wife, Sophie, and two of their three children.**

Left: **Lateiner Bridge spans the Miljacka River in Sarajevo. Archduke Franz Ferdinand's car traveled along the river to Sarajevo City Hall on June 28, 1914.**

Left: Gavrilo Princip fired two shots at the archduke and his wife, killing them both. The incident led to World War I.

THE PRINCIP MUSEUM

Today, a museum stands at the corner of Lateiner Bridge in Sarajevo, close to the site of the archduke's murder. The Princip Museum, as it is named, houses objects related to the event, including the archduke's bloodstained vest and photographs of the crime.

THE SLIDE INTO WAR

Following the death of the archduke, Germany put pressure on Austria-Hungary to declare war on Serbia. Germany's motive was to curb the military power of Russia, then the protector of Serbia. When Serbia refused to allow Austro-Hungarian police on its soil to investigate Serbian involvement in the assassination, war broke out, with Austria-Hungary, Germany, and Bulgaria siding against Serbia, Russia, and Italy. Other European powers joined in, and the crisis developed into World War I.

A Fatal Visit

On the day of the assassination, Princip and two Bosnian Serb terrorists, joined by four other would-be assassins, all stationed themselves at various points along the route that the archduke's car would take to Sarajevo City Hall. One of the men, Nedjelko Cabrinovic, threw a bomb at the archduke, but it bounced off his car and exploded beneath the vehicle behind. The assassins fled, thinking they had succeeded. Some time later, hearing that the archduke was still alive, they resumed their positions, hoping to catch the car on its way back from the function.

The archduke's publicized route had been changed because of the earlier assassination attempt, but no one had informed the archduke's driver. As the driver turned into Franz Joseph Street, he was ordered to reverse the car. Princip, who happened to be near the vehicle when it stopped, fired two shots, killing both the archduke and his wife. Both Princip and Cabrinovic were arrested, tried, and imprisoned for their acts.

Communist Rule

In 1945, the communist federation of Yugoslavia became the second largest communist regime to emerge in the world, after the Soviet Union. For nearly half a century, Bosnia was ruled as a republic within the Yugoslav federation. The federation also included Serbia, Montenegro, Croatia, Macedonia, Kosovo, Vojvodina, and Slovenia. It united, for the first time, South Slav people from the West Balkans as one political entity.

Tito's Policies

Unlike many Eastern European communist leaders, Tito pursued policies that did not always follow the Soviet line. In the 1960s, Tito's Yugoslavia adopted a policy of nonalignment, that is, of not joining either side in the Cold War between the Soviet Union and the United States. Within Yugoslavia itself, Tito departed from the Soviet model of centralized management and planning. Although his policy of "self-management" gave power to the workers and to the republics, Tito constantly restrained local autonomy and sought Yugoslav unity across the federation. He was powerful enough to hold Yugoslavia together despite tensions among the republics, but the federation gradually split up after his death.

THE RISE OF TITO

The Allies recognized Tito's Partisans as resistance fighters and aided them against Germany during World War II. In 1945, the Allies defeated the Axis powers, and Tito's forces controlled most of Yugoslavia by May. From June to November 1945, Tito consolidated his power throughout Yugoslavia by ridding his government of noncommunists and all other political opponents.

Left: **President Tito addresses an audience in the Yugoslav capital of Belgrade in 1953. Tito enjoyed tremendous popular support in Yugoslavia.**

Left: Tito's Partisans recruited boys as messengers. Bosnia played a special role in Tito's rise to power. Forced south to Herzegovina in 1943 by the Germans, the Partisans escaped to Sarajevo and finally set up their headquarters in Jajce in west-central Bosnia. Bosnians made up a significant group in the Partisans.

The Legacy of Communist Rule

Communist rule drastically changed the social, economic, and political life of Bosnia. Despite earlier attempts to clamp down on traditional Islamic institutions, in the 1960s the communist federal government recognized Bosnian Muslims not merely as a religious group but as an ethnic and national entity. Bosnian Muslims increasingly gained political power and representation. Many enrolled in the diplomatic service. Under the communist regime, the relative poverty of Bosnia compared to Serbia and Croatia prompted many Bosnian Serbs and Croats to emigrate.

The acceptance of Bosnian nationhood, however, deepened resentment in Croatia and Serbia. Both these countries had long felt that Bosnia should have been split between them rather than acknowledged as an autonomous republic within the Yugoslav federation. Thus, when Yugoslavia broke up in the early 1990s, Serbs and Croats targeted Muslims for ethnic cleansing. Rivalry among the member-republics of Yugoslavia, especially between Serbia and Croatia during Tito's rule, also intensified the rush to carve up Bosnia after the collapse of the federation. Ethnic tensions that had built up during communist rule erupted into the war of 1992–1995 and the eventual partition of Bosnia into Bosniak-Croat and Serb entities.

The Dayton Agreement

War raged in Bosnia from 1992 to 1995. International efforts to negotiate a peace settlement met with little success until the Dayton peace accord, initialed on November 21, 1995, in Ohio. The Dayton Agreement was signed on December 14, 1995, in Paris, after forty-four months of ethnic warfare.

A Divided Country

The Dayton Agreement divided Bosnia into two entities: the Bosniak-Croat Federation of Bosnia and Herzegovina and the Bosnian Serb Republika Srpska. Having separate parliaments, the two entities are fairly independent in political, economic, and social matters but defer to a central government for national policies.

The Dayton Agreement was praised for bringing together the two most militarily powerful parties in the conflict, Croatia and the Federal Republic of Yugoslavia (to which Serbia belongs). These governments agreed to withdraw their forces from Bosnia and to abandon their territorial claims to it. The U.N.-NATO Implementation Force (IFOR), since replaced by the Stabilization Force (SFOR), was given substantial military power to stop the fighting and implement the terms of the agreement.

Below: **Serbian president Slobodan Milosevic (*left*), Croatian president Franjo Tudjman (*center*), and Bosnian president Alija Izetbegovic sign the Dayton Agreement during a ceremony at Elysée Palace, Paris, on December 14, 1995. The agreement ended what many regard as Europe's worst conflict since World War II.**

Left: **The U.N. Mine Action Center in Sarajevo coordinates mine detection and clearance activities in Bosnia. It is part of international efforts to implement the peace brought about by the Dayton Agreement and to aid in Bosnia's recovery from the war of 1992–1995.**

The Dayton Agreement was also committed to helping refugees and persons displaced by the war return to their homes or claim compensation for the loss of their homes. Irrespective of ethnic identity, Bosnians were to be allowed freedom of movement in all parts of the country. War criminals were to be indicted and tried at the U.N. International Criminal Tribunal at The Hague, Netherlands. The Dayton Agreement also provided for the reconstruction of the country by establishing a transportation corporation and forming other public corporations that would provide nationwide services. A High Representative was appointed to police the implementation of the Dayton Agreement.

Despite the many systems established by the Dayton Agreement, the job of enforcing peace in Bosnia has not been easy. The greatest success of the agreement has been the end of open fighting. Many underlying tensions, however, still plague Bosnia, and several parts of the agreement remain unimplemented. For example, in practice, the Muslim-Croat and Serb entities sometimes operate independently of the central government, refusing to accommodate the return of refugees and displaced persons not belonging to their own ethnic groups. SFOR has not disarmed all paramilitary groups, and Bosnia has been accused of sheltering international terrorists. Many indicted war criminals are still at large, too, especially in Republika Srpska.

Ethnic Cleansing

The term *ethnic cleansing* refers to persecution for the purpose of ridding a territory of members of a particular ethnic group. Ethnic cleansing also seeks to erase from public memory the existence of the targeted ethnic group. In Bosnia, Serb groups embarked on the systematic destruction of all reminders of Muslim culture, from architectural monuments to historical documents.

Ethnic Hatred

Ethnic cleansing in Bosnia began in 1992, when the republic declared its independence from Yugoslavia. Serbia, using arms and equipment provided by the Yugoslav federation, wanted to claim the country for itself. Its project was to cleanse the country of Muslims and Croats. Within a few months, Serbs controlled more than 60 percent of the country. Local groups became involved in the fighting. By 1994, Bosnian Croats, supported by Croatia, joined in the Serbian bid to clear the country of Muslims. They aimed to set up a Croatian section of Bosnia.

The persecution and genocide of Muslims was the most intense in the regions of northeastern Bosnia and eastern Herzegovina. Muslims fled their hometowns in large numbers. Yugoslav federal army forces used planes to bomb many towns. Sarajevo was under

Left: At the Sasina mass grave site in western Bosnia, specialists unearthed the remains of Muslim war victims in 1996. Of the estimated 200,000 people who died in the war, 80–90 percent were Muslim civilians. Up to eight thousand Muslims are believed to lie buried in mass graves around eastern Bosnia. These burial sites continue to be found today.

Above: **Like many other buildings of Muslim heritage all over Bosnia, this mosque in Mostar was bombed during the war.**

constant siege. Muslims in Mostar were hunted first by the Serbs in 1992, and then by the Croats in 1994. Srebrenica, once the most prosperous inland town of the Balkans, was turned into a refugee camp and the site of some of the worst massacres.

Widespread Destruction

In Bijeljina and Banja Luka, all the mosques were blown up and burned to the ground. In Sarajevo, the State University Library and the Oriental Institute, which contained thousands of documents on Bosnia's Ottoman history, were destroyed by shelling. The historic town of Mostar was devastated. Its sixteenth-century Ottoman-style Old Bridge was destroyed, as was its nineteenth-century Orthodox church and its Roman Catholic church, which also had a valuable Franciscan library and archives. Today, monuments of Turkish culture lie in ruins all over Bosnia. Life in postwar Bosnia has centered largely around rebuilding these cities and monuments and helping the residents deal with the trauma of ethnic cleansing.

Historic Towns: Jajce and Banja Luka

Jajce

An attractive, medieval fortress town, Jajce is located along one of the country's most fertile and cultivated river valleys, the Vrbas. The town's mixed Slav- and Turkish-style architecture speaks of past conquests. Jajce, the capital of the Bosnian bans, fell to the Ottoman Turks with the defeat of the last monarch, Stjepan Tomasevic, in 1463. In the same year, Hungary seized Jajce and a few other territories in northern Bosnia from the Turks, establishing a mini-kingdom. The Turks retook Jajce in 1528 and controlled it for the next three and a half centuries, until Austria-Hungary regained power over Bosnia in the late nineteenth century.

After World War I, the town became part of Yugoslavia. During World War II, Tito's army, the Partisans, received the support of the

Left: **The town of Jajce is located on mountainous terrain along the Vrbas River.**

Left: The Bocka shopping mall is a popular meeting place for residents in Banja Luka. Today, Banja Luka is the capital of Republika Srpska.

Allied forces in resisting German occupation of Bosnia. Tito's communist resistance forces used Jajce as their base of operations. Today, the remains of medieval city walls, surrounding castle and watchtower ruins, still stand in Jajce.

Banja Luka

Located 29 miles (46.7 km) north of Jajce on the banks of the Vrbas River, Banja Luka has been the capital of Republika Srpska since 1998. The city was first settled by an Illyrian tribe in pre-Roman times. In 9 B.C., the Romans conquered the town. From 1583 to 1639, it was the capital of the Turkish province of Bosnia. Banja Luka was an important center for Bosnian uprisings against the Turks in the nineteenth century.

In the twentieth century, the town became a political and cultural center. Its importance, however, made it a military target and the site of much suffering and war destruction. During World War II, it was occupied by the Germans as well as by the genocidal Ustasa, a fascist Croat force that persecuted and killed Serbs, Jews, and Roma. During the war of 1992–1995, all of the town's mosques were systematically bulldozed and dynamited by the Serbs. Much Turkish-style architecture was lost, including the impressive Ferhad Pasha domed mosque, which had three mausoleums and was built in 1583.

Horror Camps of War

Omarska, Manjaca, and Trnopolje

From about May 25, 1992, prisoners started filling Omarska camp, a former mining complex approximately 9.3 miles (15 km) from the town of Prijedor in northwestern Bosnia. For three months, until about August 30, 1992, armed Serb guards confined more than three thousand Bosniaks and Bosnian Croats in Omarska under inhumane conditions.

Three different buildings were used to house prisoners and conduct camp "activities" at Omarska. Interrogations, or formal questioning sessions, took place in the administration building, which also held most of the forty women prisoners. The men were confined in the hangar building and a small building called the "white house." A cement courtyard area also held prisoners.

Below: **At Manjaca, prisoners were confined in cramped sleeping quarters. When this picture and others like it reached international attention in 1992, the world condemned the inhumane conditions in Bosnia's war camps.**

Living conditions at Omarska were shocking. Prisoners had little or no privacy and no proper bedding or medical care. They were fed rations of bread only once a day, and many had to go weeks without bathing or changing their clothes. Conditions were similar at other prison camps, such as Manjaca and Trnopolje, both also near Prijedor.

Beatings were carried out in most of the prison camps. Survivors testified that Serb guards used weapons to assault them. Many prisoners died from their injuries.

Above: **At the Trnopolje detention camp, 3,500 Bosnian Muslims and Croats were held by Bosnian Serbs for more than five months.**

Investigating War Crimes in Bosnia

In the summer of 1992, journalists brought to worldwide attention the appalling conditions at Omarska, Manjaca, and Trnopolje. Politicians and reporters who had been allowed to visit Manjaca and Trnopolje described finding prisoners huddled on dirty bedding. At Manjaca, journalists were secretly shown two prisoners with untreated wounds from beatings. Public outcry led to the closure of Omarska in August and to the creation, in 1993, of the U.N. International Criminal Tribunal for the former Yugoslavia.

Indictments and Arrests

In July 1995, the tribunal indicted Bosnian Serb leader Radovan Karadzic and his military chief, Ratko Mladic, on charges of genocide and crimes against humanity. Karadzic and Mladic were charged with cooperating in the imprisonment of thousands of non-Serbs in concentration camps like Omarska, where many prisoners died.

In 1998, the tribunal indicted the camp commander at Omarska, Zeljko Meakic, and his deputies and subordinates, accusing them of genocide, violations of the laws or customs of war, and crimes against humanity.

Major General Radislav Krstic was arrested in December 1998. The highest-ranking official to be indicted by the U.N. tribunal up to that time, Krstic was charged with personal involvement in the apparent killing of Muslim men from Srebrenica.

Today, the tribunal continues to investigate war crimes in the former Yugoslavia. As of 1998, twenty-one indictments had been made.

Music and Dance

Bosnian music, like its architecture, reflects the many cultural influences that made their way into the country over centuries. Although traditional music is heard less today, giving way to popular music, traditional melodies and musical motifs weave themselves into local pop songs. The former Yugoslav practice of resisting Westernization and promoting traditional and folk music and dance has meant that these art forms continue to be a part of Bosnian contemporary culture. Traditional music is still played on Bosnian radio today.

Bosnian music has both rural and urban traditions, with Turkish influence more strongly apparent in urban music. Rural music styles include the *ravne pjesme* (RAHV-nay PEE-es-mee), songs with flat melodies of limited vocal range. The rendition of *ganga* (GAHN-gah), songs that can be sung to more than one tune, resembles shouting more than singing. These rural songs often are accompanied by a *sargija (*SHAR-geh-yah*)*, a long-necked lute, the Bosnian wooden flute, or a *diple* (deep-LAY), a kind of bagpipe. Turkish urban songs are characterized by

Below: Local folk dancers in Sarajevo don traditional costumes to celebrate festive occasions.

"melismatic" singing, which means that there is more than one musical note per syllable, making it highly lyrical and difficult to perform. Such songs are accompanied on the *saz* (SAHZ), a more sophisticated version of the sargija. The *gusle* (GOOS-lay), a single-stringed fiddle, accompanies the singing of epic poems, an ancient tradition that has survived.

Folk Dancing

The former Yugoslav government sponsored more than four hundred amateur folklore groups in Bosnia, and traditional Bosnian folk dances are still performed today. A well-known one is the *nijemo kolo* (NEE-YAY-moh KOH-loh), which is accompanied not by music but by the stamping of feet and the jingling of silver coins on the women dancers' aprons. In line dances, the sexes are separated. Bosnian Croatian and Serbian dances resemble, respectively, those in Croatia and Serbia.

Privatizing the Economy

Bosnia's privatization program is a key component in the country's move toward a free market economy. Both the Federation of Bosnia and Herzegovina and Republika Srpska are offering formerly state-owned enterprises for sale to private individuals and businesses. The profits from the sale will help lessen foreign debt and fuel the banking sector. Privatization also means that many businesses abandoned during the war can start to operate again, offering new jobs to the unemployed. Existing enterprises are also expanding their scale of operations and hiring more workers.

Privatization is bringing foreign capital and modern business and technological expertise into the country. Bosnia's media has already benefited enormously from the privatization program. Newspapers, magazines, radio networks, and

THE OLD ECONOMY

Under the Yugoslav method of socialist self-management, business and industrial enterprises were taken over by the state. State control meant that healthy economic competition was stifled, giving rise to inefficient business management and poorly made consumer goods.

Left: **As a result of privatization, a wide range of newspapers and magazines is now available in Bosnia.**

television stations have enlarged their reach by revamping their programs. Businesses now make use of the advertising and public relations sectors when competing with others for a larger share of the market.

The privatization of the economy is radically changing the country. As businesses try to cater to the demands and needs of consumers, new products are being offered. Bosnians have become more Westernized from exposure to consumer trends in Western cities. Capitalism is also quickening the pace of life in Bosnia, as people seize new opportunities to make money.

Although privatization is taking off in Bosnia, a few obstacles remain. For instance, the Federation of Bosnia and Herzegovina and Republika Srpska have different rules concerning citizens' entitlement to buy shares and businesses. The question of whether displaced persons and refugees should participate in privatization in their previous districts or in their new homes also needs to be settled. Strong trade unions have begun to oppose the sale of enterprises, since existing workers may be fired by new owners. In order to expand its export earnings, Bosnia also needs to develop products that consumers in other countries will want to buy.

Above: **A new factory is being built in Pale. New enterprises are springing up all over Bosnia.**

The Reconstruction of Mostar

In 1997, North Atlantic Treaty Organization (NATO) divers plunged into the deep Neretva River in Mostar. They were retrieving rocks that had fallen from the Old Bridge, destroyed in 1993 by Bosnian Croatian artillery. Thus began the work of restoring the bridge that represents Mostar itself.

A Thriving Town Hit by War

The chief urban center of Herzegovina, Mostar was first mentioned in historical documents in the 1400s. The town flourished under Ottoman rule. In 1566, the Turks replaced the town's wooden bridge over the Neretva River with a stone structure. The Stari Most, which consisted of a single arch over the river, became the town's most distinctive feature. The name *Mostar* is, in fact, derived from the Serbo-Croatian word *most* (MOHST), meaning "bridge." The Ottoman town grew around the bridge. Under Austro-Hungarian rule, Mostar expanded and prospered. Its educational institutions were known as some of the best in the former Yugoslavia.

When war broke out in 1992, Mostar Croats and Bosniaks successfully defended their town against Bosnian Serbs. However, the Bosniaks turned against the Croats when the latter conquered the western part of the town to make it the capital of

Above: Mostar's Stari Most, or Old Bridge, was a magnificent example of Ottoman architecture before it was destroyed in 1993. Despite the recovery of about 60 percent of the Stari Most's stones, lack of knowledge of Ottoman workmanship will mean a broken connection with the past.

Left: A steel-framed bridge now stands in place of Tito's Bridge, which was destroyed in 1992. Originally called King Peter's Bridge, the bridge was built in 1936 and spanned the Neretva River some 0.4 mile (0.6 km) upriver from the Stari Most. King Peter's Bridge was renamed after the communists took control of Mostar in 1945.

their own republic. The Croats destroyed many symbols of Muslim culture. Industry and infrastructure were devastated and five thousand buildings damaged. About two thousand people were killed in Mostar and about 26,000 driven out.

Today, Bosniaks and Croats have settled on opposite banks of the Neretva River, separated by a "confrontation line." Most Bosnian Serbs have left the once multiethnic Mostar, and the population has been reduced to half its prewar size of 130,000.

Reconstruction of the city has been under way since 1994, supervised by the European Union Administration of Mostar (EUAM). By 1996, when the EUAM mandate ended, 30,000 people had benefited from the repair of apartments and houses. Restoration of the city's great Ottoman and Serb architectural masterpieces had also begun. Today, cafés, shops, restaurants, and dance clubs are springing up on the modern, wealthy, Croat side of the river. Nevertheless, it remains to be seen whether beautifying the confrontation line will erase Mostar residents' painful memories of ethnic hostilities.

DEALING WITH WAR TRAUMA

Psychological services have been organized for traumatized children and families. Technical and medical training centers have been set up with foreign and local universities to equip Mostar residents with knowledge and skills for the future. Cultural activities and sports have also been revived for their therapeutic power.

Sarajevo: Capital City

The region that includes Sarajevo was first settled many thousands of years ago. By the mid-thirteenth century, the area was an important administrative, trading, and artistic center of the medieval state of Bosnia. The Ottoman Turks established this area as a city in the mid-fifteenth century. The name *Sarajevo* first appeared in 1477 in a historical document written in Arabic. The Ottomans developed Sarajevo as a model Islamic city that revolved around Bosnia's biggest bazaar.

In 1697, forces from Austria-Hungary attacked and destroyed the town, but the Turks rebuilt it. Sarajevo continued to expand in the late 1800s, during the period of Austro-Hungarian rule. In the twentieth century, however, the city has been plagued by unrest. It was in Sarajevo that Bosnian Serb Gavrilo Princip assassinated Franz Ferdinand, heir apparent to the Austro-Hungarian throne, setting World War I in motion. In 1992, Bosnian Serbs who refused to recognize the newly independent government in Sarajevo mounted a four-year siege of the city, killing and wounding many.

Below: **Residential communities are settled on the hillsides surrounding the Sarajevo city center. In addition to numerous domed mosques, Sarajevo has a sixteenth-century Eastern Orthodox church and a synagogue. A major fire in 1639 and another in 1879 — the first full year of Austro-Hungarian rule — permitted the Europeanization of Sarajevo's architecture and accounts for the unique blend of Eastern and Western styles in the city.**

During the siege, the central boulevard, Zmaja od Bosne, was known as "Snipers' Alley." The grand suburb of Dobrinja, built as the athletes' village for the 1984 Winter Olympics, was a front line in the war. Over 11,000 residents were killed and more than 61,000 wounded.

Trauma and a sense of loss linger beneath the restored surface beauty of the city today. A U.S. $5-billion restoration effort has patched up shelled buildings, but the city's former energy has yet to return. Before the war, the city was multiethnic in character. Today, however, the 350,000 inhabitants are mostly poor Bosniaks, many of them refugees who fled ethnic cleansing in Serb areas. Only 20 percent of the city's original inhabitants remain. Sarajevo's prewar Croat and Serb populations have been uprooted and moved either to their own ethnic areas in other parts of Bosnia or to neighboring Croatia and Serbia. Nevertheless, the civilians of Sarajevo are gradually resuming control of the city from SFOR and other international agencies. Events such as the annual Sarajevo Film Festival and the Sarajevo Poetry Days show that the city's cultural scene is very much alive.

Above: **Sarajevo residents walk in the now-peaceful streets of the city. A U.S. $5-billion restoration effort has helped beautify Sarajevo since its historic buildings suffered extensive damage during the war.**

SFOR: Keeping the Peace

Before SFOR: IFOR

On December 16, 1995, two days after the signing of the Dayton Agreement in Paris, NATO launched a large-scale operation to implement the military terms of the peace settlement. A NATO-led multinational force called the Implementation Force (IFOR) began its one-year mission in Bosnia on December 20. Numbering about 60,000, IFOR succeeded in its aims to end all fighting and separate the armed forces of the Federation of Bosnia and Herzegovina from those of Republika Srpska. IFOR patrolled the 870-mile (1,400-km) long demilitarized boundary between the two entities. It also repaired and made main transportation lines safe for use.

Transition to SFOR

When the IFOR mandate expired, NATO leaders judged Bosnia still in need of a peacekeeping force. The Stabilization Force (SFOR) was activated on December 20, 1996. The difference in roles between SFOR and IFOR is reflected in their names: while

Left: **SFOR soldiers load their weapons in Doboj in 1998. SFOR is charged with maintaining the peace implemented by IFOR.**

the role of IFOR had been to implement peace, the task of SFOR is to stabilize Bosnia and preserve a secure environment in which local and national governments and international organizations can operate.

Above: **Portuguese soldiers take a break in a café in Sarajevo. These men form part of the international peacekeeping force in Bosnia.**

SFOR supports civilian institutions in charge of implementing the terms of the peace settlement. These organizations include the Office of the High Representative, the International Police Task Force, the U.N. High Commission for Refugees, the Organization for Security and Cooperation in Europe, and the International Criminal Tribunal for the former Yugoslavia. SFOR has assisted in the arrest of indicted war criminals in Bosnia.

An International Effort

Like IFOR, SFOR is made up of troops from eighteen NATO nations with armed forces. Iceland, the only NATO nation which does not have armed forces, is providing medical aid. In addition, sixteen non-NATO nations, including Finland, Ireland, Russia, and Sweden, have contributed troops to SFOR. In this way, the Bosnian peace process is resulting in truly international cooperation and support.

The White Countryside

There is something surreal, or dreamlike, about the karst countryside of southwestern Bosnia. The effect is particularly striking in the areas surrounding Mostar in Herzegovina, where the lush greenery of the city, with its mulberry, fig, and oleander trees, contrasts with the surrounding harsh and unrelenting landscape of barren limestone rocks, caves, underground rivers, and sinkholes.

What Is Karst Terrain?

Although karst terrain can be found in other parts of the world, including France, China, and, in the United States, the Midwest, Kentucky, and Florida, the term was first used for the soluble limestone terrain of the Dalmatian coast of the Adriatic Sea.

Rain dissolves the soft limestone found in this landscape, deepening cracks along joints and producing a jagged and grooved terrain. When rainwater drains along the vertical and horizontal cracks in dense limestone in the surface layers of soil, it creates underground streams and rivers and cave systems. If rain dissolves a major portion of the limestone above a large cave, the cave ceiling may collapse, forming a sinkhole. Sinkholes are common in Herzegovina. When many join together, a *polja*

Left: **Rainfall creates vertical grooves in the limestone rock in Bosnia's karst countryside. Water flows down these channels into underground springs.**

(POH-lyah) — a large depression covered with the insoluble remains of limestone — forms. In karst regions, polje are the only places suitable for the cultivation of crops.

The Popovo Polje, or "Priest's Countryside," stretches some 40 miles (64 km) southeast of Mostar and is typical of karst landscape. Reportedly a Turkish battle site and the site of a pre-Roman state, the area is now barren and filled with yellowish-gray rocks. Flocks of sheep wander this region, surviving on thistles and other weeds. Foxes, jackals, and the occasional bush are perhaps the only other easily visible forms of life to inhabit the area. In summer, the landscape is parched and dry. In winter, however, underground streams and rivers flood; their waters reach the surface and, as if by magic, form a large lake.

"Rock-born" rivers are another unusual phenomenon. These rivers spring from the face of a cliff, then disappear underground, only to reemerge some distance away. When they surface, the rivers create a surprisingly fertile area rich in vegetation.

The geographical features of karst landscapes may interest travelers, but native Bosnians are less thrilled by them. Karst terrain does not encourage settlement. Because rainfall in these regions disappears into underground rivers and streams most of the year, the land is not suitable for cultivation, and villagers are unable to get adequate water even for domestic purposes.

The Women of Bosnia and Herzegovina

The position of women in Bosnia tends to vary from place to place and according to ethnicity. Muslim women are considered the most conservative among Bosnian women. Yet, perhaps because of Bosnia's more European outlook and influences, Islam in Bosnia does not place the same restrictions on Bosnian Muslim women that apply to women in the Middle East and parts of Asia. For instance, Bosnian women do not wear a veil and are not confined to special women-only parts of the house. The sexes also mingle freely at social events. Urban Muslim women have absorbed many Western and modern influences and often cannot be distinguished from urban Serb and Croat women in their dress. Bosnian Serb and Croat women have largely abandoned traditional ethnic costumes, except on certain festive occasions.

Toward Equality with Men

Social changes during the years of Tito's rule helped establish women's independence. Since communism demanded that women play a larger role in the economic life of the federation, their social

Left: **Bosnian Muslim girls walk past election rally posters on a street in eastern Mostar in September 1998. More conservative Muslim women still wear headscarves and long skirts or traditional baggy trousers. Many urban Bosnian Muslim women, however, have adopted modern, Western dress.**

RELATIONS WITH NORTH AMERICA

Close relations between North America and Bosnia are a twentieth-century development. North American forces helped liberate the Balkans from Germany in both world wars. Despite U.S. distrust of communism in the 1950s and 1960s, Yugoslav leader Josip Broz Tito visited then U.S. president John F. Kennedy at the White House in Washington, D.C., in 1963. Since the outbreak of war in 1992, the United States and Canada have been committed to providing military and humanitarian aid to Bosnia. U.S. participants played key roles in negotiating the Dayton peace settlement. The 10th Mountain Division of the U.S. Army now heads SFOR, the international peacekeeping force in Bosnia. SFOR helps refugees and displaced persons reconstruct their homes. The U.S. and Canada are also assisting in the cultural rebuilding of Bosnia, as academics from all three countries work together to create an electronic collection of valuable Bosnian manuscripts destroyed during the war of 1992–1995.

Opposite: **U.S. president Bill Clinton, accompanied by General William Nash, commander of U.S. ground forces in Bosnia, walks through the ranks at Tuzla air base on January 13, 1996.**

Below: **The North American soft drink Coca-Cola and other Western products are readily available in Bosnia.**

Left: Allied troops fought in the Balkans in World War I. British, French, Serbian, Italian, and Greek forces defeated Bulgaria, which sided with the Central Powers. The United States joined the war on the side of the Allies in 1917.

World War I

Until the early twentieth century, relations between Bosnia and the United States had been peaceful but distant. In 1914, however, a conflict began that would eventually draw in both countries. When Archduke Franz Ferdinand of Austria-Hungary was assassinated in Sarajevo by a Bosnian Serb, Gavrilo Princip, Austria-Hungary declared war on Serbia. The United States initially declared itself neutral. U.S. president Woodrow Wilson tried to negotiate a peace settlement between the Allies (then mainly Britain, France, and Russia), who were backing Serbia, and the Central Powers (mainly Austria-Hungary, Germany, and Turkey). In 1917, however, Germany resorted to unrestricted submarine warfare against all shipping to Britain, including U.S. ships. Seeing this move as a violation of U.S. rights as a neutral party, the U.S. government broke relations with Germany on April 6, 1917, and entered World War I on the side of the Allies. In 1918, U.S. troops played a vital role in defending French territories from Germany, speeding the eventual surrender of the Central Powers.

Yugoslav Communism

During World War II, German forces occupied Bosnia. The Partisans, led by Josip Broz Tito, fought against the Germans in Bosnia and other Balkan countries. Britain and the United States viewed Tito's army as a resistance movement and provided it with military assistance against Germany. In 1945, Tito succeeded in freeing Bosnia. Bosnia became a republic in the communist-ruled Yugoslav federation, which included Slovenia, Croatia, Serbia, Macedonia, and Montenegro.

Relations between the United States and Bosnia (then part of Yugoslavia) cooled in the postwar years as rivalry between the United States and the Soviet Union grew. The U.S. government increasingly distrusted Yugoslavia because of Tito's suspected communist ties with the Soviet Union. The truth, however, was that Yugoslavia maintained its autonomy from the Soviet Union. In fact, Tito's relations with the Soviet leader Josef Stalin were so bad that, by the late 1940s, Stalin tried but failed to replace the Yugoslav regime with a government that he could control.

Conflict with the Soviet Union and distrust by the United States led to Tito's policy of nonalignment with either power. In the 1950s, Tito found like-minded leaders in Gamal Abdel Nasser of Egypt and Jawaharlal Nehru of India. In 1961, Tito sponsored the first meeting of nonaligned states in Belgrade, the Yugoslav capital. The Nonaligned Movement continued until the 1990s, when the disintegration of the Soviet Union led to a new period of improved U.S.-Russian relations.

Left: **Tito (*center*) gives a speech during his visit to the White House in Washington, D.C., on October 21, 1963. Listening to him are then U.S. president John F. Kennedy (*left*); Kennedy's wife, Jackie (*center back*); and Tito's wife, Herta Haas (*right*). Tito tried to steer a middle course between the Soviet Union and the United States.**

Peace Brokers

In the early years of the war in Bosnia, the European Community attempted to negotiate for peace, but the warring factions rejected any kind of settlement. Despite the U.S. government's cautious approach to intervening in the war in Bosnia, U.S. and Canadian troops were sent, from the beginning of the war, to enforce peace and preserve Bosnia's independence. Eight hundred Canadian soldiers formed part of the United Nations force in Bosnia. In three-and-a-half years, at a cost of Can $1 billion, Canadians flew more than one thousand aid missions to Bosnia using Hercules planes.

With the entry of the United States as a peace broker in 1994, hostilities between Croats and Bosniaks ceased. Air attacks by NATO forces persuaded the Serbs to consider ending the war. In early 1995, former U.S. president Jimmy Carter managed to negotiate a cease-fire that lasted for four months. The war finally ended with the signing of a U.S.-brokered peace accord, the Dayton Agreement, at the end of 1995.

Below: **Former U.S. president Jimmy Carter (*far left*) listens to the then president of Republika Srpska, Radovan Karadzic (*far right*), at a meeting in Pale in December 1994. Carter managed to negotiate a four-month cease-fire for the whole of Bosnia.**

The Dayton Agreement

The Dayton Agreement is not seen as the perfect solution to ethnic conflicts in Bosnia. Many Bosnians in North America and at home did not want a country split into two ethnic parts and governments. Nevertheless, as Bosnian president Alija Izetbegovic remarked at the time, the peace that the agreement brought was more just than continued warfare.

Today, the United States and Canada are committed to implementing the terms of the Dayton Agreement. These include bringing Yugoslav war criminals to justice and returning refugees to their homes.

North Americans were represented in the Implementation Force (IFOR) that enforced and preserved peace in Bosnia in 1995. IFOR has since been replaced by the Stabilization Force, SFOR, which has much the same peacekeeping role. Europe, Russia, and the United States are currently in the process of launching a new regional order in the Balkans in the form of a Stability Pact that will encourage economic reconstruction and regional cooperation.

Above: **President Slobodan Milosevic of Serbia, President Alija Izetbegovic of Bosnia, President Franjo Tudjman of Croatia, and U.S. Secretary of State Warren Christopher** *(seated from left to right)* **initial a peace accord at the Hope Hotel at Wright-Patterson Air Force Base, Dayton, Ohio, on November 21, 1995. The Dayton Agreement was signed in Paris the following month.**

Immigration to North America

Before the wars involving the breakup of Yugoslavia, few Bosnians migrated to North America. When they did, they classified themselves as Yugoslavs.

During the war, Bosnian migrant communities in the West proved to be a potent force, motivating North Americans to give assistance to Bosnia. They raised public awareness of the ethnic cleansing taking place in the western Balkans and sought to bring their relatives and friends to North America. Some Bosnian-Canadians and Bosnian-Americans organized themselves, respectively, as the Friends of Bosnia Society (Ottawa) and the Community of Bosnia (Philadelphia).

A majority of Bosnians who migrate to either the United States or Canada are Bosniaks. Since the war of 1992–1995, an estimated 150,000 Bosniaks have entered both countries as refugees. They identify themselves as Bosnians, while Bosnian Serbs and Bosnian Croats generally prefer to identify with long-established North American Serb and Croat communities rather than with Bosnians.

Below: **Members of the Serb community in Ottawa, Canada, demonstrate against the NATO bombing of Yugoslavia, which includes Serbia, Kosovo, Vojvodina, and Montenegro, in 1999. Air strikes were ordered after Yugoslav troops brutally suppressed ethnic Albanian efforts to create an independent Kosovo. Ottawa is home to a large Balkan population. Bosnian Serbs tend to identify with the local Serb community rather than with local Bosnians.**

Left: **Sarajevan cellist Vedran Smaljovic (*left*) and his sister, Violeta Smaljovic of Dallas, Texas, gave a concert at the Statue of Liberty in New York Harbor on January 24, 1995. Their performance raised awareness of the war in Bosnia. Today, Bosnians, Bosnian-Americans, and Bosnian-Canadians continue to work together and with U.S. and Canadian organizations, supplying Bosnia with humanitarian aid.**

Friends of Bosnia

Bosnian immigrants see Canada as the Western country that most welcomes them. Friends of Bosnia is a Canadian nonprofit organization that has given financial and other aid to Bosnia during the war. It also helps Bosnian refugees settle in Canada and integrate into local society. Friends of Bosnia provides scholarships for students studying Bosnian history and is helping to rebuild library and archival collections of Bosnian culture. Politically, it favors a multiethnic and united, democratic Bosnia.

The Community of Bosnia

The Community of Bosnia was founded in Haverford, Pennsylvania. It enables needy and deserving Bosnian students to attend high schools and colleges in the United States. The organization also provides these students with psychotherapy for war trauma and helps them adjust to life in the United States. After completing their education, the students return to Bosnia to share with others what they have learned in the United States. Members of the Community of Bosnia, some of whom are university professors, speak up internationally against genocide and ethnic cleansing.

USAID

The U.S. Agency for International Development (USAID) administers and manages the U.S. national program to assist other countries. The agency is given an annual budget of U.S. $6 billion to fund assistance projects in more than seventy-five countries. With the end of the Cold War and the dismantling of socialist governments in Eastern Europe, Congress approved a program called SEED (Support for Eastern European Democracy), which authorized USAID to promote the transition of former socialist countries into democratic systems of government and to aid their operation as free market economies. Bosnia is one of thirteen countries to receive a portion of the funds allotted to this project.

Several major objectives guide USAID activities in Bosnia. The agency seeks to help rebuild industrial and other facilities damaged by the war and to restore services, such as health care, that were disrupted by ethnic troubles. USAID also plays an important role in helping the Bosnian government privatize state-owned industries. USAID advisers are involved in developing new laws required for the privatization of businesses and industry, and the agency provides training for government officials, business managers, and the media in accounting and administrative procedures involved in privatization.

AIDING PRIVATIZATION

USAID offers U.S. $5 million in loans every month to enable individuals and enterprises in Bosnia to take over state-owned companies. USAID estimates that it creates about five hundred jobs a month by doing this.

Left: **This playground in Sarajevo was built with USAID funds.**

Regathering Bosnian Manuscripts

The Oriental Institute in Sarajevo, which housed one of the most important collections of Islamic manuscripts in the world, was destroyed by Serb forces in May 1992. The Serbs wanted to remove all traces of Bosnian Islamic cultural heritage. Almost all of the institute's precious collection went up in flames, including tens of thousands of Ottoman-era documents and about five thousand bound manuscripts in Arabic, Persian, Turkish, and Hebrew.

The original documents are lost forever, but the Oriental Institute's long-term friendly relations with university and national libraries abroad is now working in its favor. When approached for information, the institution, set up in 1950, always readily offered copies of original Islamic documents. Now, it is trying to gather some of these copies to make up an electronic collection of the original manuscripts. Institute staff have gone to all quarters of the world looking for these copies. They are also trying to track down copies of manuscripts in private collections. Canadian and U.S. academics from leading universities, such as Harvard and the Massachusetts Institute of Technology, have come to their assistance.

Above: Vijecnica, the national and university library in Sarajevo, was burned on August 25, 1992. Although it was later repaired, many valuable manuscripts and books were lost. North Americans are trying to restore collections of manuscripts from libraries and archives destroyed in Bosnia during the war. The Library of the Museum of Herzegovina and the Archives of Herzegovina were among the institutions that lost precious historical documents.

Helping Refugees Return Home

Many Bosnians were displaced from their hometowns by the war and were forced to resettle in other areas, especially in refugee camps. The better educated were able to migrate to other countries. International and state efforts now focus on helping refugees return to their homes. Only proper housing, however, and the availability of work near their former homes can persuade the refugees to return. The restoration of electrical power and water supplies, control of industrial pollution, and help in rebuilding homes, as well as the arrival of new businesses in the area, have brought a small percentage of the refugees back.

USAID power projects have restored electricity to about one quarter of Bosnia's population. The agency estimates that its activities contributed to bringing back some 80,000 refugees. The agency was involved in rehabilitating the Kakanj power plant and has also helped install environmental protection equipment that drastically reduced pollution by the plant. This project benefited the 850,000 people who lived in the area, as well as local industry

Above: **U.N. soldiers help villagers in Maklenovac, Bosnia, rebuild their homes.**

and businesses. In Usora, USAID took part in a project that brought water to all of the municipality's 9,000 residents. It also invested nearly U.S. $2 million in bringing electricity to Doboj's 30,000 residents.

Center for Civic Initiatives (CCI)

U.S. funds also have helped Bosnian civic organizers return displaced people to their homes. The lonely nature of rebuilding their entire lives after the war discourages many refugees from returning home. Believing that these refugees are better motivated and strengthened when they work in groups, the Center for Civic Initiatives (CCI) helps refugees to form groups to rebuild their communities. Former residents of Doljani and Sovici are among groups CCI has helped. CCI also trains grassroots organizations, or groups of ordinary citizens to improve the lives of their communities by participating in the political process. Bosnians learn to speak and act on behalf of their communities in their dealings with local governments, making it easier for refugees to return home.

Below: **Bosnian Muslim refugees sit outside their tent home on an airfield in Tuzla, waiting to return to their hometowns. More than two million people, largely Serbs and Muslims, were displaced from their hometowns. Most do not expect to return to their homes despite the provisions of the Dayton Agreement.**

BOSNIA AND HERZEGOVINA

SLOVENIA

HUNGARY

● ZAGREB

Sava

CROATIA

Una

● Bihać

Prijedor ● ● Trnopolje

Omarska ●

Sasina ● ● Manjaca

● Banja Luka

Maklenovac ●

Vrbas

Sava Bosanski Šamac

Bosna

● Doboj

Vojvodina

Danube

● Usora

Tuzla ●

● Bijeljina

Sava

BELGRADE ●

BOSNIA (region)

● Jajce

Bosna

● Travnik

● Kakanj

● Zvornik

Drina

Serbia

Srebrenica ●

YUGOSLAVIA

SARAJEVO ■

● Pale

Visegrad ●

Busko Jezero

Doljani ●

Jablanicko Jezero

Jablanica ●

HERZEGOVINA
(region)

Foča ●

● Sinj

Dalmatian Coast

Sovici ●

Mostar ●

● Stolac

Medjugorje ●

Neretva

Gacko ●

▲ Mount Maglic
(7,828 ft / 2,386 m)

Montenegro

Kosovo

Dubrovnik ●

N

ADRIATIC SEA

ALBANIA

———	State Boundary
- - - -	Regional Boundary
———	Entity Boundary
▧	Republika Srpska
	Federation of Bosnia and Herzegovina
■	Capital
●	City
～～	River

Above: Residents of Sarajevo enjoy relaxing in the Old Town area of the city.

Adriatic Sea A4–C5
Albania D5

Banja Luka B2
Belgrade (Serbia) D2
Bihać A2
Bijeljina C2
Bosanski Šamac C2
Bosna River C2–C3
Bosnia (region) A2–C4
Busko Jezero (lake) B3

Croatia A1–C5

Dalmatian coast A3–C5
Danube River C1–D2
Dinaric Alps A2–D5
Doboj C2
Doljani B3
Drina River C4–D2
Dubrovnik (Croatia) C4

Federation of Bosnia
and Herzegovina
A2–C4
Foča C3

Gacko C4

Herzegovina (region)
B3–C4
Hungary B1–C1

Jablanica B3
Jablanicko Jezero
(lake) B3
Jajce B3

Kakanj C3
Kosovo D4–D5

Maklenovac C2
Manjaca B2
Medjugorje B4
Montenegro C4–D5
Mostar B4
Mount Maglic C4

Neretva River B4–C4

Omarska B2

Pale C3
Prijedor B2

Republika Srpska A2–C4

Sarajevo C3
Sasina B2
Sava River A1–D2
Serbia D2–D4
Sinj (Croatia) A3
Slovenia A1
Sovici B4
Srebrenica D3
Stolac B4

Travnik B3
Trnopolje B2

Tuzla C2

Una River A3–B2
Usora C2

Visegrad D3
Vojvodina C1–D2
Vrbas River B2–B3

Yugoslavia C1–D5

Zagreb (Croatia) A1
Zvornik C2

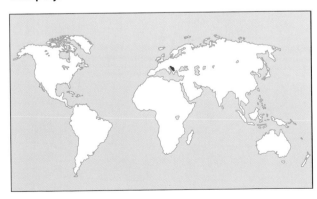

BOSNIA AND HERZEGOVINA

How Is Your Geography?

Learning to identify the main geographical areas and points of a country can be challenging. Although it may seem difficult at first to memorize the locations and spellings of major cities or the names of mountain ranges, rivers, deserts, lakes, and other prominent physical features, the end result of this effort can be very rewarding. Places you previously did not know existed will suddenly come to life when referred to in world news, whether in newspapers, television reports, or other books and reference sources. This knowledge will make you feel a bit closer to the rest of the world, with its fascinating variety of cultures and physical geography.

Used in a classroom setting, the instructor can make duplicates of this map using a copy machine. (PLEASE DO NOT WRITE IN THIS BOOK!) Students can then fill in any requested information on their individual map copies. Used one-on-one, the student can also make copies of the map on a copy machine and use them as a study tool. The student can practice identifying place names and geographical features on his or her own.

Above: **Farmers gather at a sheep market in Sarajevo.**

Bosnia and Herzegovina at a Glance

Official Name	Republic of Bosnia and Herzegovina
Capital	Sarajevo
Official Language	Serbo-Croatian (Bosnian, Croatian, or Serbian)
Population	3,482,495 (1999 estimate) *Note: All population data is subject to variation due to dislocations caused by military action and ethnic cleansing.*
Land Area	19,781 square miles (51,233 square km)
Administrative Divisions	Federation of Bosnia and Herzegovina, Republika Srpska
Highest Point	Mount Maglic at 7,828 feet (2,386 m)
Main Rivers	Bosna, Drina, Neretva, Sava, Una, Vrbas
Main Religions	Eastern Orthodox Christianity, Islam, Roman Catholicism
Ethnic Groups	Bosniak (Muslim), Croat, Serb
National Holidays	Federation of Bosnia and Herzegovina — Republic Day (November 25)
	Republika Srpska — Republic Day (January 9), Independence Day (March 1)
Flag	The flag of Bosnia and Herzegovina features a yellow triangle on a blue background. Running across the flag and parallel to the longest side of the triangle are seven full five-pointed stars and two half stars, at the top and bottom edges of the flag.
Industries	Bauxite, coal, domestic appliances, iron ore, lead, manganese, oil refining, steel, tank and aircraft assembly, textiles, tobacco products, vehicle assembly, wooden furniture
Currency	Convertible Mark (2.192 BAK = U.S. $1 as of 2000)

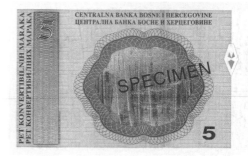

Opposite: **Jajce is located close to a waterfall on the Vrbas River.**

Glossary

Serbo-Croatian Vocabulary

badnjak (BAHD-nyak): a Yule log.

bans (BAHNS): in medieval times, Bosnian viceroys under Hungarian authority. In practice, however, the Bosnian bans acted independently, often resisting their Hungarian rulers.

bezistan (BEZZ-ih-stahn): domed structures that house textile shops.

bosanski lonac (BOSS-ahn-skee LON-atz): a layered stew consisting of meat and vegetables.

cevapcici (CHAY-VAHP-chee-chee): ground meat seasoned with spices and shaped into sausages.

devsirme (DEV-seer-mee): the child-tribute system used by the Ottoman Turks to train citizens of conquered territories for service in the Ottoman military or administration.

diple (deep-LAY): a kind of bagpipe.

ganga (GAHN-gah): songs with more than one tune.

gusle (GOOS-lay): a single-stringed fiddle.

ide na kafu (ih-deh nah KAH-FOO): coffee visit; a time when friends or neighbors visit and chat.

kefir (KAY-fir): a thin yogurt drink.

loza (LOH-zzah): grape brandy.

moreska (MOR-res-kah): a 400-year-old Croatian dance drama.

most (MOHST): a bridge.

nijemo kolo (NEE-YAY-moh KOH-loh): a dance accompanied by the stamping of feet and the jingling of silver coins on the women dancers' aprons.

pljeskavica (PLYAY-skah-vit-zah): ground meat seasoned with spices and shaped into patties.

polja (POH-lyah): in limestone plateaus, a depression that contains fertile river deposits.

polje (POH-lyeh): the plural of *polja*.

ravne pjesme (RAHV-nay PEE-es-mee): songs with flat melodies of limited vocal scale.

salep (SAH-lape): a type of tea.

sargija (SHAR-geh-yah): a long-necked lute.

saz (SAHZ): a kind of lute.

sevdalinka (SEV-DAHL-een-kah): traditional love songs.

sljivovica (SHLEE-voh-vit-zah): plum brandy.

somun (SOH-moon): a thick pita bread.

English Vocabulary

activists: people who take action for political causes.

amateur (adj.): engaged in an activity for enjoyment rather than financial gain.

annexed: added to the domain of a country.

apparitions: visions.

atrocities: extremely wicked or brutal acts.

baroque: a style of art and architecture of the early seventeenth to mid-eighteenth century, characterized by rich forms that suggest movement.

bombarded: attacked with bombs or gunfire.

capitalism: an economic system in which businesses are owned and maintained chiefly by private individuals or groups.

chamois: an agile goatlike antelope that lives in mountainous parts of Europe.

coalition (adj.): relating to a union of two or more parties.

communist: relating to a system of government in which all property is state- or community-owned; a person who supports such a system.

constitution: the system of laws according to which a country is governed.

cosmopolitan: sophisticated.

elite: the best of a group or class.

encrustation: the addition of rich materials to a surface.

entities: distinct units.

ethnic cleansing: the elimination of an unwanted ethnic group from society.

fascist: relating to a system of government that is led by a dictator and that emphasizes aggressive nationalism; a person who supports such a system.

feminist (adj.): relating to a movement that advocates rights for women equal to those of men.

filigree: delicate ornamental work.

genocide: the deliberate and systematic extermination of a political, racial, cultural, or religious group.

Gothic: a style of architecture of the mid-twelfth to sixteenth century, characterized by pointed arches and rich ornamentation.

homogeneous: consisting of elements that are all of the same kind.

humanitarian aid: help given to improve the welfare and happiness of people.

illumination: the art of decorating manuscripts with gold, silver, and intricate designs.

indicted: charged with a crime or crimes.

karst: an area of limestone terrain characterized by sinkholes, ravines, and underground streams.

mandate: an order or a command.

mausoleums: stately tombs.

megaliths: large stones, especially those in ancient constructions.

minarets: tall, slender towers attached to mosques.

nationalism: devotion and loyalty to one's own nation.

paramilitary: an organization that operates in a manner resembling a regular military force.

privatization: the act of selling state-owned industries to private individuals or groups.

puppet state: a state that is independent in name but is actually controlled by a foreign power.

ragout: a highly seasoned stew.

secular: nonreligious.

socialist: relating to a system of government in which the means of production and distribution are state-controlled; a person who supports such a system.

terrorism: the use of violence for political purposes.

therapeutic: relating to the restoration of physical or mental well-being.

trauma: shock or severe distress produced by violent disturbances, such as war.

tribunal: a court of justice.

tributaries: streams that flow into larger streams or other bodies of water.

tripartite: divided into or consisting of three parts.

More Books to Read

Bosnia: Can There Ever Be Peace? Topics in the News series. David Flint (Raintree Steck-Vaughn)

Bosnia: Civil War in Europe. Children in Crisis series. Keith Elliot Greenberg (Blackbirch Marketing)

Bosnia: Fractured Region. World in Conflict series. Eric Black (Lerner)

Bosnia: The Struggle for Peace. Sherry Ricciardi (Millbrook Press)

A Bosnian Family. A Journey Between Two Worlds series. Robin Landew Silverman (Lerner)

Life in War-Torn Bosnia. The Way People Live series. Diane Yancey (Lucent Books)

Scar on the Stone: Contemporary Poetry from Bosnia. Chris Agee (Dufour Editions)

The Visions of the Children: The Apparitions of the Blessed Mother at Medjugorje. Janice T. Connell (St. Martin's Press)

The War in Former Yugoslavia. New Perspectives series. Nathaniel Harris (Raintree Steck-Vaughn)

Young People from Bosnia Talk About War. Issues in Focus series. Harvey Fireside and Bryna J. Fireside (Enslow)

Zlata's Diary: A Child's Life in Sarajevo. Zlata Filipovic (Penguin)

Videos

For the Children of Bosnia. (UNI/London Classics)

The Great War and the Shaping of the 20th Century. (PBS Home Video)

While America Watched — Bosnia T. (MPI Home Video)

Web Sites

www.bosnet.org/

www.bosnia.org.uk/news

www.bosnianembassy.org

www.oxfam.org.uk/coolplanet/kidsweb/world/Bosnia/boshome.htm

Due to the dynamic nature of the Internet, some web sites stay current longer than others. To find additional web sites, use a reliable search engine with one or more of the following keywords to help you locate information about Bosnia. Keywords: *Ivo Andric, Bosnians, Dayton Agreement, Alija Izetbegovic, karst, Medjugorje, Mostar, Omarska, Sarajevo, SFOR.*

Index